MAY OUR PEOPLE TRIUMPH

Patrice Lumumba

Poem, Speeches, Letters and Interview of Congo's Revolutionary Prime Minister   Patrice Lumumba

LEOPARD BOOKS.COM

May our People Triumph – Patrice Lumumba

Prepared for Publication by:
Paul Daniel Aravinth

Published by:

LEOPARD BOOKS
http://LeoPardBooks.com

ISBN-10: 1530766192
ISBN-13: 978-1530766192

Printed by **CreateSpace**, an *Amazon.com* Company

Our Print Books and E-Books are available at
http://amazon.com and all Amazon sites, Kindle store,
http://LeoPardBooks.com, Kobo and all leading
International online book stores & E-Book stores

Search Terms: "Sankar Srinivasan"

Contents

Biography of Patrice Lumumba
(1925-1961)

Lumumba was the first Prime Minister of the Democratic Republic of the Congo.

He was born in Kasai province of the Belgian Congo. He was educated at a missionary school and worked in Leopoldville (Kinshasa) and Stanleyville (Kisangani) as a clerk and journalist. In 1955 Lumumba became regional president of a Congolese trade union and joined the Belgian Liberal Party. He was arrested in 1957 on charges of embezzlement and imprisoned for a year. On his release he helped found the Mouvement National Congolais (MNC) in 1958. In 1959 Belgium announced a five year path to independence and in the December local elections the MNC won a convincing majority despite Lumumba being under arrest at the time. A 1960 conference in Belgium agreed to bring independence forward to June 1960 with elections in May. Lumumba and the MNC formed the first government on June 23, 1960, with Lumumba as Prime Minister and Joseph Kasavubu as President.

His rule was marked by the political disruption when the province of Katanga declared independence under Moise Tshombe in June 1960 with Belgian support. Despite the arrival of United Nations troops unrest continued and Lumumba sought Soviet aid. In September Lumumba was dismissed from government by Kasavubu, an act of dubious legality. On September 14 a coup d'etat headed by Colonel Joseph Mobutu (later Mobutu Sese Seko) and supported by Kasavubu gained power. Lumumba was arrested on December 1, 1960 by troops of Mobutu. He was captured in Port Francqui and flown to Leopoldville in handcuffs. Mobutu said Lumumba would be tried for inciting the army to rebellion and other crimes. United Nations Secretary General Dag Hammarskjold made an appeal to Kasavubu asking that Lumumba be treated according to due process of law. The USSR denounced Hammarskjold and the Western Powers as responsible for Lumumba's arrest and demanded his release.

The United Nations Security Council was called into session on December 7 to consider Soviet demands that the U.N. seek Lumumba's immediate release, the immediate restoration of Lumumba as head of the Congo government, the disarming of the forces of Mobutu, and the immediate evacuation of Belgians from the Congo. Soviet Representative Valerian Zorin refused U.S. demands that he disqualify himself as Security Council President during the debate. Secretary General Dag Hammarskjöld, answering Soviet attacks against his Congo operations, said that if the U.N. force were withdrawn from the Congo "I fear everything will crumble."

Following a U.N. report that Lumumba had been mistreated by his captors, his followers threated (on December 9) to arrest all Belgians and "start cutting off the heads of some of them" unless Lumumba was released within 48 hours.

The threat to the U.N. cause was intensified by the announcement of the withdrawal of their U.N. Congo contingents by Yugoslavia, the United Arab Republic, Ceylon, Indonesia, Morocco, and Guinea. The Soviet pro-Lumumba resolution was defeated on December 14 by a vote of 8-2. On the same day, a Western resolution that would have given Hammarskjold increased powers to deal with the Congo situation was vetoed by the Soviet Union.

Lumumba was then transported on January 17, 1961 from the military prison in Thysville near Leopoldville to a "more secure" prison in Jadotville in the Katanga Province. There were reports that Lumumba and his fellow prisoners, Maurice Mpolo and Joseph Okito, were beaten by provincial police upon their arrival in secessionist Katanga.

Two months later, Lumumba was executed along with his two aides.

In February of 2002, the Belgian government admitted to "an irrefutable portion of responsibility in the events that led to the death of Lumumba."

In July of 2002 documents released by the United States government revealed that the CIA had played a role in Lumumba's assassination, aiding his opponents with money and political support, and in the case of Mobutu with weapons and military training. [from Wikipedia]

May our People Triumph

Poem by Patrice Lumumba

Weep, O my black beloved brother deep buried in eternal, bestial night.

O you, whose dust simooms and hurricanes have scattered all over the vast earth, You, by whose hands the pyramids were reared

In memory of royal murderers, You, rounded up in raids; you, countless times defeated In all the battles ever won by brutal force;

You, who were taught but one perpetual lesson, One motto, which was—slavery or death; You, who lay hidden in impenetrable jungles

And silently succumbed to countless deaths Under the ugly guise of jungle fever, Or lurking in the tiger's fatal jaws, Or in the slow embrace of the morass

That strangled gradually, like the python....

But then, there came a day that brought the while, More sly, more full of spite than any death.

Your gold he bartered for his worthless beads and baubles, He raped and fouled your sisters and your wives, And poisoned with his drink your sons and brothers, And drove your children down into the holds of ships.

'Twas then the tomtom rolled from village unto village, And told the people that another foreign slave ship Had put off on its way to far-off shores Where God is cotton, where the dollar reigns as King.

There, sentenced to unending, wracking labour, Toiling from dawn to dusk in the relentless sun, They taught you in your psalms to glorify Their Lord, while you yourself were crucified to hymns

That promised bliss in the world of Hereafter, While you—you begged of them a single boon:

That they should let you live—to live, aye—simply live. And by a fire your dim, fantastic dreams Poured out aloud in melancholy strains, As elemental and as wordless as your anguish.

It happened you would even play, be merry And dance, in sheer exuberance of spirit: And then would all the splendour of your manhood, The sweet desires of youth sound, wild with power,

On strings of brass, in burning tambourines.

And from that mighty music the beginning Of jazz arose, tempestuous, capricious, Declaring to the whites in accents loud That not entirely was the planet theirs.

O Music, it was you permitted us To lift our face and peer into the eyes Of future liberty, that would one day be ours.

Then let the shores of mighty rivers bearing on Their living waves into the radiant future, O brother mine, be yours!

Let the fierce heat of the relentless midday sun Burn up your grief!

Let them evaporate in everlasting sunshine, Those tears shed by your father and your grandsire Tortured to death upon these mournful fields.

And may our people, free and gay forever, Live, triumph, thrive in peace in this our Congo, Here, in the very heart of our great Africa!

Patrice Lumumba

Source: **Patrice Lumumba, The Truth about a Monstrous Crime of the Colonialists**, Moscow, Foreign Languages Publishing House, 1961, pp. 48-49. **Written:** by Patrice Lumumba; **Transcribed:** by Thomas Schmidt.

Address to Congolese Youth

Patrice Lumumba, August, 1960

Today I am addressing the youth, the young men and women of the Republic of the Congo.

In speaking to them, I am addressing these words to future generations because the future of our beloved country belongs to them.

We are fighting our enemies in order to prepare a better and happier life for our youth.

If we had been egoists, if we had thought only about ourselves we would not have made the innumerable sacrifices we are making.

I am aware that our country can completely liberate herself from the chains of colonialism politically, economically and spiritually only at the price of a relentless and sometimes dangerous struggle. Together with the youth of the country, we have waged this struggle against foreign rule, against mercantile exploitation, against injustice and pressure.

Young people who have been inactive and exploited for a long time have now become aware of their role of standard-bearer of the peaceful revolution.

The young people of the Congo have fought on our side in towns, villages and in the bush. Many of our young men have been struck down by the bullets of the colonialists. Many of them left their parents and friends in order to fight heroically for the cause of freedom. The resistance that the young people offered the aggressors in Leopoldville on January 4 and in Stanleyville on October 30, 1959, deserves every praise.

With deep emotion I bow in memory of these courageous patriots, these fighters for African freedom.

The time is not far distant when large numbers of young men and women were driven out of schools by their white teachers and instructors on the suspicion of having nationalist ideas. Many brilliantly gifted young people turned down the opportunity to receive a higher education for the simple reason that they no longer wished to be indoctrinated by the colonialists, who wanted to turn our young men and women into eternal servants of the colonial regime.

During the heroic struggle of the Congolese nationalists, the young people, even those who were still sitting at school desks, resolutely opposed all new forms of colonialism, whether political, social, spiritual or religious.

Their only dream was national liberation. Their sole aim was immediate independence.

Their only resolve was to wage an implacable struggle against the puppets and emissaries of the colonialists.

Thanks to the general mobilisation of all the democratic youth of the Congo, the Congolese nationalists won independence for the nation. We received this independence at the price of a grim struggle, at the price of all sorts of privations, at the price of tears and blood.

After independence was solemnly proclaimed on June 30, 1960, the colonialists and their black emissaries started a barbarous war in the young Republic of the Congo. They began this perfidious aggression because the nationalist Government now in power did not want them to continue exploiting our country as they did prior to June 30, the historic day when the people of our country said *Adieu* to the Belgian colonialists.

Not having any support whatever, particularly among the working class, who have had their fill of colonial exploitation, the colonialists and their henchmen now want to force certain sections of the youth to serve them in order to be able to propagandise the revival of colonialism. That is why a certain part of the youth, luckily not a very numerous part, have plunged into national defeatism.

Happily, the vast majority of the young people saw through this last attempt of the imperialists, who are turning into account the dissatisfaction of some malcontents, of those who failed in the elections because they did not have the confidence of the people.

This nationalist youth recently held demonstrations in various towns in the Republic to show their absolute and total opposition to imperialist intrigues.

Young people, I salute you, and congratulate you on your civic and patriotic spirit. Young people, especially for you I have created a Ministry for Youth Affairs and Sports under the Central Government. It is your Ministry. It is at your disposal. Many of you, without any discrimination, will be called upon to direct this Ministry, its different services and activities.

Today, in the free and independent Congo we must not have a Bangala, National Unity Party, Association of Bakongo, Mukongo, Batetela or Lokele youth but a united, Congolese, nationalist, democratic youth. This youth will serve the social and economic revolution of our great and beloved country.

You must energetically combat tribalism, which is a poison, a social scourge that is the country's misfortune today. You must combat all the separatist manoeuvres, which some of the preachers of the policy of division are trying to pass off to young and inexperienced people under the name of federalism, federation or confederation.

In reality, young people, these names are only a new vocabulary brought by the imperialists to divide us in order the better and more conveniently to exploit us. Your entire future will be threatened if you do not oppose these manoeuvres, this new, disguised colonisation.

You must be proud that you belong to a great nation, a great country, a mighty power. This power, which the imperialists envy today, is embodied in national unity. This unity must be the heritage that you, in your turn, shall leave to your children.

The Government will soon send 300 young people to study in the U.S.A., 150 in the Soviet Union and 20 in Guinea, not to mention other countries.

The Congo is no longer a national reservation, a national park, a zoo which we could not leave. Tomorrow you shall go everywhere to study, to learn a speciality, and to get to know the world. Workers, working people will have an equal share in these study missions.

You shall go everywhere, to all the parts of the world. These contacts with the outside world, this direct confrontation with the reality of life will make you experienced people, whom the free and independent Congo needs today.

You will go there not as representatives of Association of Bakongo, National Unity Party, Congo National Movement or African Regroupment Centre youth. You will be Congolese citizens, simply Congolese. And by your behaviour, devotion, intelligence and political maturity you must be a credit to your Congolese motherland.

Young people, the Congo belongs to you. The national Government, the people's Government will do everything in its power to prevent the Congo from being torn away from you.

Long live the Republic of the Congo!

Long live the people's, democratic youth!

Source: Patrice Lumumba: Fighter for Africa's Freedom
Moscow, Progress Publishers, 1961, pp 33-36. **Written:** *by Patrice Lumumba;* **Transcribed:** *by Thomas Schmidt.*

Speech at the opening of the All-African Conference in Leopoldville

Patrice Lumumba, August 25, 1960

Prime Minister Patrice Lumumba speaks at the opening of the All-African Conference in Leopoldville, August 25, 1960

Ministers, Ladies and gentlemen, Dear comrades,

The fighting Congolese people are proud and happy to receive their brothers-in-arms in their country today.

For my Government, for us Congolese, your presence here at such a moment is the most striking proof of the African reality whose existence our enemies have always denied and are still attempting to deny. But you, of course, know that that reality is even more stubborn than they, and Africa lives on and fights. She refuses to die to justify the arguments about the backwardness of our history, a history we have made with our hands, our skins and our blood.

It is at conferences such as this that, we first became conscious of our personality, of our growing solidarity. When at our first conferences, which were held in various cities in Africa, we brought up the problem of decolonisation the imperialists never expected we would be successful. However, since the first Conference of the Peoples of Africa in Accra in December 1958 we have traversed the entire road of the liberation of our continent together.

You will recall the upsurge of the liberation struggle of the peoples of Angola, Algeria, the Congo, Kenya, Mozambique, Nyasaland and Rhodesia after the Conference in Accra, and of Ruanda-Urundi today. You will remember that a decisive step forward was taken after that historic Conference. Nothing, neither bullets, nor repressions, could stop this popular movement.

The work of this Conference is aimed at accelerating the movement for the independence of the African continent.

Ministers, dear fighters for the freedom of Africa, it is your duty to show the world and those who sneer at us that nothing can deter us from liberating Africa, which is our *common* aim.

We can achieve this aim only in solidarity and unity. Our solidarity will have meaning only when it is boundless and when we are convinced that Africa's destiny is indivisible.

Such are the deep-going principles of the work you will have to do. This meeting will prepare the ground for a Summit Conference at which our countries will have to speak on:

1) The unqualified support of all the African states in the general struggle for a Pan-African bloc;

2) A policy of neutralism with the purpose of achieving genuine independence;

3) The breaking down of colonial barriers through cultural exchanges;

4) Trade agreements between the African states;

5) Africa's position with regard to the European Common Market;

6) Military co-operation;

7) The building in Leopoldville of a powerful radio station with the aid of all the African states;

8) The creation of a research centre in Leopoldville.

Ministers, you have come into contact with the reality of the Congo here, in the very heart of the crisis that we shall have to resolve.

Your confidence in the future of our continent will unquestionably help you to complete your work successfully. Your principal purpose is to prepare a meeting of our Heads of State, who will indeed establish African unity, for whose sake you have responded to our appeal.

You know the origin of what is today called the Congolese crisis, which is actually only a continuation of the struggle between the forces of pressure and the forces of liberation. At the very outset of the Belgian aggression, my Government, the guarantor and representative of the sovereignty of the Congolese nation, decided to appeal to the United Nations. The U.N. has responded. And so has the free world. Belgium has been condemned. I went to New York to show world public opinion the moving forces of the Congolese drama.

Upon our return from the United States we replied to the invitation of the Heads of the free African states, who publicly adopted a definite position and unanimously extended to us their fraternal support. From this rostrum I express my gratitude to President Bourguiba, His Majesty Mohammed V, President Sekou Toure, President Tubman, President Nkrumah and President Olympio, whom I had the honour to meet at this decisive moment. I regret that material difficulties prevented me from replying to the invitation of President Nasser and His Majesty Haile Selassie.

All of them, fighting for African unity, have said "No" to the strangulation of Africa. All of them immediately realised that the attempts of the imperialists to restore their rule threaten not only the independence of the Congo but also the existence of all the independent states of Africa. They all realised that if the Congo perishes, the whole of Africa will be plunged into the gloom of defeat and bondage.

That is further striking proof of African unity. It is concrete testimony of the unity that we need in the face of imperialism's monstrous appetite.

All statesmen are agreed that this reality is not debated but fought for so that it may be defended.

We have gathered here in order that together we may defend Africa, our patrimony. In reply to the actions of the imperialist states, for which Belgium is only an instrument, we must unite the resistance front of the free and fighting nations of Africa. We must oppose the enemies of freedom with a coalition of free men. Our common destiny is now being decided here in the Congo.

It is, in effect, here that the last act of Africa's emancipation and rehabilitation is being played. In extending the struggle, whose primary object was to save the dignity of the African, the Congolese people have chosen independence. In doing so, they were aware that a single blow would not free them from colonial fetters, that juridical independence was only the first step, that a further long and trying effort would be required. The road we have chosen is not an easy one, but it is the road of pride and freedom of man.

We were aware that as long as the country was dependent, as long as she did not take her destiny into her own hands, the main thing would be lacking. This concerns the other colonies, no matter what their standard of life is or what positive aspects of the colonial system they have.

We have declared our desire for speedy independence without a transition period and without compromises with such emphasis because we have suffered more mockery, insults and humiliation than anybody else.

What purpose could delays serve when we already knew that sooner or later we would have to revise and re-examine everything? We had to create a new system adapted to the requirements of purely African evolution, change the methods forced on us and, in particular, find ourselves and free ourselves from the mental attitudes and various complexes in which colonisation kept us for centuries.

We were offered a choice between liberation and the continuation of bondage. There can be no compromise between freedom and slavery. We chose to pay the price of freedom.

The classical methods of the colonialists, which we all knew or partially still know, are particularly vital here: survivals of military occupation, tribal disunity, sustained and encouraged over a long period, and destructive political opposition, planned, directed and paid.

You know how difficult it has been for a newly independent state to get rid of the military bases installed by the former occupying powers. We must declare here and now that henceforth Africa refuses to maintain the armed forces of the imperialists in its territory. There must be no more Bizertes, Kitonas, Kaminas and Sidi Slimanes. We have our own armies to defend our countries.

Our armed forces, which are victims of machinations, are likewise freeing themselves from the colonial organisation in order to have all the qualities of a national army under Congolese leadership.

Our internal difficulties, tribal war and the nuclei of political opposition seemed to have been accidentally concentrated in the regions with our richest mineral and power resources. We know how all this was organised and, in particular, who supports it today in our house.

Our Katanga because of its uranium, copper and gold, and our Bakwanga in Kasai because of its diamonds have become hotbeds of imperialist intrigues. The object of these intrigues is to recapture economic control of our country.

But one thing is certain, and I solemnly declare that the Congolese people will never again let themselves be exploited, that all leaders who will strive to direct them to that road will be thrown out of the community.

The resonance that has now been caused by the Congolese problem shows the weight that Africa has in the world today. Our countries, which only yesterday they wanted to ignore as colonial countries, are today causing the old world concern here in Africa. Let them worry about what belongs to them. That is not our affair. Our future, our destiny, a free Africa, is our affair.

This is our year, which you have witnessed and shared in. It is the year of our undisputed victory. It is the year of heroic, blood-drenched Algeria, of Algeria the martyr and example of struggle. It is the year of tortured Angola, of enslaved South Africa, of imprisoned Ruanda-Urundi, of humiliated Kenya.

We all know, and the whole world knows it, that Algeria is not French, that Angola is not Portuguese, that Kenya is not English, that Ruanda-Urundi is not Belgian. We know that Africa is neither French, nor British, nor American, nor Russian, that it is African.

We know the objects of the West. Yesterday they divided us on the level of a tribe, clan and village. Today, with Africa liberating herself, they seek to divide us on the level of states. They want to create antagonistic blocs, satellites, and, having begun from that stage of the cold war, deepen the division in order to perpetuate their rule.

I think I shall not be making a mistake if I say that the united Africa of today rejects these intrigues. That is why we have chosen the policy of positive neutralism, which is the only acceptable policy allowing us to preserve our dignity. For us there is neither a Western nor a communist bloc, but separate countries whose attitude towards Africa dictates our policy towards them. Let each country declare its position and act unequivocally with regard to Africa.

We refuse to be an arena of international intrigues, a hotbed and stake in the cold war. We affirm our human dignity of free men, who are steadily taking the destiny of their nations and their continent into their own hands.

We are acutely in need of peace and concord, and our foreign policy is directed towards co-operation, loyalty and friendship among nations. We want to be a force of peaceful progress, a force of conciliation. An independent and united Africa will make a large and positive contribution to world peace. But torn into zones of hostile influence, she will only intensify world antagonism and increase tension.

We are not undertaking any discriminative measures. But the Congo is discriminated against in her external relations. Yet in spite of that she is open for all and we are prepared to go anywhere. Our only demand is that our sovereignty be recognised and respected.

We shall open our doors to specialists from all countries motivated by friendship, loyalty and co-operation, from countries bent not on ruling Africans but on helping Africa. They will be welcomed with open arms.

I am sure that I shall be expressing the sentiments of all my African brothers when I say that Africa is not opposed to any nation taken separately, but that she is vigilant against any attempt at new domination and exploitation both in the economic and spiritual fields. Our goal is to revive Africa's cultural, philosophical, social and moral values and to preserve our resources. But our vigilance does not signify isolation. From the beginning of her independence, the Congo has shown her desire to play her part in the life of free nations, and this desire was concretised in her request for admission to the United Nations.

Ministers and dear comrades, I am happy to express the joy and pride of the Government and people of the Congo at your presence here, at the presence here of the whole of Africa. The time of projects has passed. Today Africa must take action. This action is being impatiently awaited by the peoples of Africa. African unity and solidarity are no longer dreams. They must be expressed in decisions. United by a single spirit, a single aspiration and a single heart, we shall turn Africa into a genuinely free and independent continent in the immediate future.

Long live African unity and solidarity!

Forward, Africans, to complete liberation!

Patrice Lumumba

Source: Patrice Lumumba: Fighter for Africa's Freedom,
Moscow, Progress Publishers, 1961, pp 19-25. **Written:** *by Patrice*
Lumumba; **Transcribed:** *by Thomas Schmidt.*

Concluding speech at the All-African Conference in Leopoldville

August 31, 1960

Your Excellencies, Delegates, Ladies and gentlemen, Dear comrades,

On behalf of the Government and people of the Republic of the Congo we salute you for the magnificent work that you have done.

Solemnly opened on August 25 under the banner of solidarity, the All-African Conference, which we invited to Leopoldville, has successfully completed its work. You have worked as a team in a spirit of understanding and have placed the interests of Africa above our individual interests and features. The success of this Conference gives us grounds for believing in Africa's future. Africa's unity will not be possible until all her children become united among themselves.

This has been profoundly grasped by us and that is why we are here together in this hall.

We have only just completed a tour of the interior of the Republic. We were accompanied by delegates from African countries and by African and foreign journalists, whom we invited. Everybody has seen the enthusiasm of the people and their trust in their Government and leaders. Everybody has seen how the Congolese trust their African brothers and how sincere the inhabitants of our country are in their striving for peace and order. Everybody could see the real face of the Congo and its people.

The colonialists have created a false problem. It is, as you know, the Katanga drama, which conceals an entire headquarters of saboteurs of our national independence. This headquarters, which at present operates covertly, through intermediaries, has the sole object of stirring up trouble, creating difficulties for the Government, discrediting it abroad through carefully organised propaganda, and re-enslaving the Congo. And all this for the sole purpose of securing their own interests.

The colonialists care nothing for Africa for her own sake. They are attracted by African riches and their actions are guided by the desire to preserve their interests in Africa against the wishes of the African people. For the colonialists all means are good if they help them to possess these riches.

Luckily for us, the Congolese people and their Government have shown themselves to be vigilant. Our struggle is aimed at liberating the country, restoring peace and consolidating social justice.

The Congo became independent under conditions which did not exist in any other African country. In other places the transition from the colonial regime to independence had intermediate stages, in the Congo everything preceded differently. We gained our sovereignty without any intermediate stage. One single step took us from one hundred per cent colonial dependence to one hundred per cent independence.

We took over the country's leadership on June 30, 1960, and only a few days later, without giving us time to organise ourselves, the Belgian Government used a false pretext to launch flagrant aggression against us. We replied to these acts of provocation and force by appealing to the United Nations.

In so doing the Government of the Republic wished to avoid war and the extension of disorders in the Congo. We placed our trust in the United Nations, convinced that it would be able to come to our assistance.

Our endless appeals to that international organisation and the many trips that members of the Government and I have undertaken to U.N. Headquarters in New York bear out how much we desire the incidents in the Congo to be stopped peacefully.

The only reason for any divergence of opinion between the Government of the

Republic and the U.N. Secretary-General is that in all their actions in the Congo, contrary to the resolutions of the Security Council, the representatives of the United Nations never consulted us.

These incidents could have been avoided if from the very beginning there had been a spirit of co-operation between representatives of the United Nations and the Government of the Republic. We have never tried to cast a doubt on the work that the United Nations is doing in Africa.

Who will deny that the joint efforts of the United Nations prevented many disasters in the world?

Who will deny that for many long years the colonial peoples placed their hopes in the United Nations?

We ourselves have appealed to the United Nations many times during our struggle against the Belgian colonialism.

On behalf of the Government and people of the Republic of the Congo we confirm our trust in the U.N. and in the different nations composing it. Our greatest desire is that this organisation should pursue its aims with greater efficacy for the happiness of mankind. The Government of the Republic will not stint any effort to help maintain peace and international security.

We have solemnly appealed to the National Army and the forces of the United Nations to combine their efforts in their mission to pacify the country.

Agreement between United Nations representatives in the Congo and the Government of the Republic is absolutely indispensable. It would facilitate harmony and understanding between U.N. troops and the Congolese army.

We salute the magnificent work the United Nations is doing in the Congo today.

We thank all the countries which have responded to our appeal and continue to render us all possible aid.

Many countries have spared no effort to help the Congo with food, medicines, materials and other forms of aid.

I cannot pass over in silence the fact that the Congolese appreciate the gestures of human solidarity from the friends of our freedom.

Similarly, we pay tribute to troops of the National Army for their fidelity. They are serving the Republic with a civic spirit and patriotism.

From the very outset of these events, our troops have known no rest and their ideal is to serve the Republic, their country, to defend the people and the integrity of the Republic, and they are prepared to die for this ideal. They are possessed with the idea of entering Katanga without delay and liberating their brothers. They burn with impatience. This consciousness of our soldiers is encouraging the entire people.

The Congo, dear delegates from the African countries, is inhabited by a peace-loving people, but they have decided to defend the unity of their beloved country. They are person who really want peace and order and stretch out their hand to everybody who sincerely wishes to help them.

Europeans of goodwill, Belgians of good intentions will always find a friendly welcome in our country. We want to turn the Congo into a great, free and flourishing nation, into a land of democracy and freedom. We are profoundly inspired by the trust that the African states are showing us today, and you may be sure, dear delegates, that we shall do everything in our power to justify that trust.

The solidarity that you have demonstrated by gathering in Leopoldville today is a vivid lesson for our people. That is why we are making a fraternal appeal for unity to all our compatriots. Unity alone can help and save us. We are very proud to note today that this has been excellently understood by the Congolese people.

Since Africa is showing her solidarity with regard to us, we, in our turn, must be more united than ever before. It is this unity, dear brothers in struggle, dear brothers in poverty, that strengthens us and enables us to hold out against the intrigues and plots of the colonialists.

The presence in Leopoldville of representatives of all African countries is helping the cause of Africa. The Western world has realised that it can no longer continue its game without the risk of completely losing Africa's friendship.

The Western world now appreciates the value that Africa attaches to her freedom and dignity. It has realised that if it wants to live in friendship with Africa it must respect Africa's dignity and rights.

That is the decisive step that has been taken today towards the speedy and complete liberation of Africa and her normal co-operation with the rest of the world. Peace will not be complete in Africa until the West stops its colonial activities.

We declare that the Government and people of the Congo have no hate or hostility for Belgium or any other European nation. And yet no sooner had the Belgian Government announced the withdrawal of its troops from Katanga than it replaced them with other troops. They include, for example, the hundred

Belgian gendarmes recently arrived in Katanga under the guise of "technical advisers", who will "teach" and "train" Tshombe's police.

Moreover, before leaving Elisabethville, General Gheysen, commander of the Belgian occupation force in Katanga, demanded the creation of a neutral zone between Kasai and Katanga and the neutralisation of the bases in Kamina and Kitona. The Belgian general did not limit himself to recommendations. He took action. The roads, bridges and strategic points in Katanga were mined under the direction of the Belgian army and on direct instructions from the Government in Brussels.

At the same time, the entire white population in Katanga was put in a state of mobilisation. Every European received a mobilisation notification signed by the commander of the Volunteer Corps and the Belgian Territorial Administrator.

I shall read you the official mobilisation order.

"Kabalo Territory,

"Volunteer Corps,

"Mobilisation Order:

"M. Gerard Vanderschrick,

"ATA, Kabalo

"An additional 25 cartridge clips have been made available for your weapon.

"Your mission is:

"To remain at the Territory Bureau, where you will be at the disposal of the Commander of the Volunteer Corps, who will give you your assignment in patrol or guard duty.

"Before reporting to the Territory Bureau you have sufficient time (fifteen minutes after the receipt of this order) to take your family to the Hotel Verret—which has been set aside for non-combatants—where they will be assured the necessary protection. You are to take with you a suitcase with clothes, a water filter, pots and a minimum supply of food.

"Commander, Volunteer Corps,

"J. Bruhiere.

"Territory Administrator,

"H. Callens."

This document has been turned over to the press.

The Volunteer Corps is a military organisation created and maintained by the Belgian Government. It has demonstrated its resolute unwillingness to leave Katanga.

The object of this manoeuvre of the Belgian Government is quite obvious: if, for the sake of appearances, it officially withdraws its troops it will, in reality, strengthen and reinforce its occupational potential by sending other military personnel under the guise of "technicians" and mobilising all Belgian nationals residing in Katanga. On behalf of the Government and people of the Congo, we are making it clear that it is not a matter of neutralising the bases at Kamina and Kitona, but of their total and complete evacuation.

We do not want any foreign military base in the Congo, even if it is controlled and maintained by the United Nations.

Not a single square metre of Congolese territory must belong to any foreign power, and nothing can and must be done in our country without the permission of its Government, which is the custodian of the legality and sovereignty of the Congolese people.

We are simply a people who have suffered long from abasement of our dignity and our rights. We are a patient people.

We know that nothing durable can be achieved by continued rancour, and we therefore demand that the Belgians and their allies stop all activity engendering disunity and hostility.

The Government, supported by the people, will soon begin exploiting the country's wealth with the aid of a vast programme of investments.

Political independence has no meaning if it is not accompanied by rapid economic and social development. We can achieve this progress only by tireless effort. With our own hands we shall soon build up our own economy.

The Government of the Republic of the Congo shall make an effective contribution to enable Africa to liberate herself immediately from foreign rule. We ardently desire to see the rejuvenation of Africa despite our regional, language and philosophical differences and the difference in manners and customs.

A free Africa, a united Africa, an undivided Africa, a determined Africa will play a great role in creating a better world, a fraternal world. Such, Your Excellencies and dear delegates, are the thoughts and profound hopes of the people and Government of the Republic of the Congo.

We wish all of you a happy return home and ask you to be our intermediaries in conveying to your governments and people our sincere gratitude for the support you have given us in this period of ordeal that we are living through.

United as the children of one family, we shall defend the honour and freedom of Africa.

Long live African independence and solidarity! Long live the union of independent African states!

Source: *Patrice Lumumba: Fighter for Africa's Freedom*, *Moscow, Progress Publishers, 1961, pp 26-33*. **Written:** *by Patrice Lumumba;* **Transcribed:** *by Thomas Schmidt.*

Speech at the ceremony of the proclamation of the Congo's Independence

Patrice Lumumba, June 30, 1960

Men and women of the Congo, Victorious independence fighters,

I salute you in the name of the Congolese Government.

I ask all of you, my friends, who tirelessly fought in our ranks, to mark this June 30, 1960, as an illustrious date that will be ever engraved in your hearts, a date whose meaning you will proudly explain to your children, so that they in turn might relate to their grandchildren and great-grandchildren the glorious history of our struggle for freedom.

Although this independence of the Congo is being proclaimed today by agreement with Belgium, an amicable country, with which we are on equal terms, no Congolese will ever forget that independence was won in struggle, a persevering and inspired struggle carried on from day to day, a struggle, in which we were undaunted by privation or suffering and stinted neither strength nor blood.

It was filled with tears, fire and blood. We are deeply proud of our struggle, because it was just and noble and indispensable in putting

Page 45

an end to the humiliating bondage forced upon us.

That was our lot for the eighty years of colonial rule and our wounds are too fresh and much too painful to be forgotten.

We have experienced forced labour in exchange for pay that did not allow us to satisfy our hunger, to clothe ourselves, to have decent lodgings or to bring up our children as dearly loved ones.

Morning, noon and night we were subjected to jeers, insults and blows because we were "Negroes". Who will ever forget that the black was addressed as *"tu"*, not because he was a friend, but because the polite *"vous"* was reserved for the white man?

We have seen our lands seized in the name of ostensibly just laws, which gave recognition only to the right of might.

We have not forgotten that the law was never the same for the white and the black, that it was lenient to the ones, and cruel and inhuman to the others.

We have experienced the atrocious sufferings, being persecuted for political convictions and religious beliefs, and exiled from our native land: our lot was worse than death itself.

We have not forgotten that in the cities the mansions were for the whites and the tumbledown huts for the blacks; that a black was not admitted to the cinemas, restaurants and shops set aside for "Europeans"; that a black travelled in the holds, under the feet of the whites in their luxury cabins.

Who will ever forget the shootings which killed so many of our brothers, or the cells into which were mercilessly thrown those who no longer wished to submit to the regime of injustice, oppression and exploitation used by the colonialists as a tool of their domination? All that, my brothers, brought us untold suffering.

But we, who were elected by the votes of your representatives, representatives of the people, to guide our native land, we, who have suffered in body and soul from the colonial oppression, we tell you that henceforth all that is finished with.

The Republic of the Congo has been proclaimed and our beloved country's future is now in the hands of its own people.

Brothers, let us commence together a new struggle, a sublime struggle that will lead our country to peace, prosperity and greatness.

Together we shall establish social justice and ensure for every man a fair remuneration for his labour.

We shall show the world what the black man can do when working in liberty, and we shall make the Congo the pride of Africa.

We shall see to it that the lands of our native country truly benefit its children.

We shall revise all the old laws and make them into new ones that will be just and noble.

We shall stop the persecution of free thought. We shall see to it that all citizens enjoy to the fullest extent the basic freedoms provided for by the Declaration of Human Rights.

We shall eradicate all discrimination, whatever its origin, and we shall ensure for everyone a station in life befitting his human dignity and worthy of his labour and his loyalty to the country.

We shall institute in the country a peace resting not on guns and bayonets but on concord and goodwill.

And in all this, my dear compatriots, we can rely not only on our own enormous forces and immense wealth, but also on the assistance of the numerous foreign states, whose co-operation we shall accept when it is not aimed at imposing upon us an alien policy, but is given in a spirit of friendship.

Even Belgium, which has finally learned the lesson of history and need no longer try to oppose our independence, is prepared to give us its aid and friendship; for that end an agreement has just been signed between our two equal and independent countries. I am sure that this co-operation will benefit both countries. For our part, we shall, while remaining vigilant, try to observe the engagements we have freely made.

Thus, both in the internal and the external spheres, the new Congo being created by my government will be rich, free and prosperous. But to attain our goal without delay, I ask all of you, legislators and citizens of the Congo, to give us all the help you can.

I ask you all to sink your tribal quarrels: they weaken us and may cause us to be despised abroad. I ask you all not to shrink from any sacrifice for the sake of ensuring the success of our grand undertaking.

Finally, I ask you unconditionally to respect the life and property of fellow-citizens and foreigners who have settled in our country; if the conduct of these foreigners leaves much to be desired, our Justice will promptly expel them from the territory of the republic; if, on the contrary, their conduct is good, they must be left in peace, for they, too, are working for our country's prosperity.

The Congo's independence is a decisive step towards the liberation of the whole African continent. Our government, a government of national and popular unity, will serve its country.

I call on all Congolese citizens, men, women and children, to set themselves resolutely to the task of creating a national economy and ensuring our economic independence.

Eternal glory to the fighters for national liberation! Long live independence and African unity! Long live the independent and sovereign Congo!

Source: *Patrice Lumumba, The Truth about a Monstrous Crime of the Colonialists*, Moscow, Foreign Languages Publishing House, 1961, pp. 44-47. **Written**: by Patrice Lumumba; **Transcribed**: by Thomas Schmidt.

Correspondence

From a letter to Dag Hammarskjöld, U.N.
Secretary-General, July 26, 1960

New York, July 20, 1960

I am informing you of the following facts: 50 soldiers have been shelled in Shinkolobwe, seven soldiers have been killed in Jadotville, 40 soldiers have been killed in Elisabethville and 12 soldiers have been killed in Kolwezi.

The Minister of Justice reports that thousands of Congolese citizens have been fired on in Kipushi, Dilolo, Bukama, Manono, Kabalo, Albertville, Kabongo, Kamina and Kaniamba. In addition, European settlers are killing all Congolese appearing singly on the highways.

This report has come from the general of our national army Mr. Victor Lundula.

The Minister of Justice of our republic informs us that the Belgian troops, now being withdrawn from the other provinces of the Congo, are concentrating in Katanga Province, where they have their headquarters. The Minister insists on the unconditional and immediate withdrawal of Belgian troops from the entire territory of the country.

In view of the gravity of the situation, I permit myself to insist once again on the following demand that was forwarded to you earlier: "Belgian troops must be immediately withdrawn from the Congo."

I ask you to inform the members of the Security Council of these new facts from the Congo.

P. LUMUMBA, Prime Minister

From a telegram to Dag Hammarskjöld, U.N. Secretary-General, August 5, 1960

I am happy the U.N. has decided to send troops to Katanga. I am aware that with the help of cunning manoeuvres inspired by Belgian officers, whom the Government of Brussels has assigned to Tshombe, the Belgian Government has attempted to ignore the decisions of the United Nations. I firmly hope you will not give in to the blackmail of the Government of Belgium through its puppet Tshombe. I cannot understand how Dr. Bunche could go to Katanga to discuss with Tshombe the question of the arrival of U.N. troops in that province. Such negotiations with a member of a provincial government contradict the decisions of the Security Council.

The Security Council had, after all, instructed you to take the necessary steps, in consultation with the Government of the Congo, to render us such military assistance as we may require. You should, therefore, negotiate with our Government and not with Tshombe. In an effort to retain its troops in Katanga with the purpose of stabilising the split it has provoked, the Belgian Government asserts that its troops were sent to Katanga Province on Tshombe's request.

With that decision the Belgian Government admits that it initiated the breakaway of Katanga Province. In its resolution of July 22, the Security Council called upon all states to refrain from any action that might hinder the restoration of public order and the exercise of authority by the Congolese Government. Similarly, it requested these states to refrain from any action that might undermine the territorial integrity and the political independence of the Republic of the Congo. By placing its troops and military advisers at Tshombe's disposal to facilitate the splitting up of the Congo and to obstruct the actions of the United Nations, the Belgian Government openly hinders the restoration of public order in the Congo and the exercise of authority by the Congolese Government.

Patrice LUMUMBA, Prime Minister

From a letter to **Dag Hammarskjöld, U.N. Secretary-General, August 14, 1960**

As it has informed Mr. Bunche, the Government of the Republic of the Congo can in no way agree with your personal interpretation, which is unilateral and erroneous. The resolution of July 14, 1960, explicitly states that the Security Council authorises you "to provide the Government (of the Republic of the Congo] with such military assistance as may be necessary". This text adds that you are to do so "in consultation with" my Government. It is, therefore, clear that in its intervention in the Congo the United Nations is not to act as a neutral organisation but rather that the Security Council is to place all its resources at the disposal of my Government.

From these texts it is clear that contrary to your personal interpretation, the United Nations force may be used "to subdue the rebel Government of Katanga", that my Government may call upon the United Nations services to transport civilian and military representatives of the Central Government to Katanga in opposition to the provincial Government of Katanga and that the United Nations force has the duty to protect the civilian and military personnel representing my Government in Katanga.

Paragraph 4 of the Security Council's resolution of August 9, 1960, which you invoke in order to challenge this right, cannot be interpreted without reference to the two earlier resolutions. This third resolution which you cite is only a supplement to the two preceding resolutions, which remain unaltered. The resolution to which you refer confirms the first two. It reads: "... confirms the authority given to the Secretary-General by the Security Council resolutions of July 14 and July 22, 1960, and requests him to continue to carry out the responsibility placed on him thereby."

It follows from the foregoing that Paragraph 4 which you invoke cannot be interpreted as nullifying your obligations to "provide the Government with such military assistance as may be necessary" throughout the entire territory of the Republic, including Katanga. On the contrary, it is the particular purpose of this third decision of the Security Council to make it clear that Katanga falls within the scope of the application of the resolution of July 14, 1960.

My Government also takes this opportunity to protest against the fact that upon your return from New York en route to Katanga, you did not consult it, as prescribed in the resolution of July 14, 1960, despite the formal request submitted to you by my Government's delegation in New York before your departure and despite my letter replying to your cable on this subject. On the contrary, you have dealt with the rebel Government of Katanga in violation of the Security Council's resolution of July 14, 1960.

That resolution does not permit you to deal with the local authorities until after you have consulted with my Government. Yet you are acting as though my Government, which is the repository of legal authority and is alone qualified to deal with the United Nations, did not exist. The manner in which you have acted until now is only retarding the restoration of order in the Republic, particularly in the Province of Katanga, whereas the Security Council has solemnly declared that the purpose of the intervention is the complete restoration of order in the Republic of the Congo (see the resolution of July 22, 1960).

Furthermore, the talks you have just had with Mr. Moise Tshombe, the assurances you have given him and the statements you have just made to the press are ample evidence that you are making yourself a party to the conflict between the rebel Government of Katanga and the legal Government of the Republic, that you are intervening in this conflict and that you are using the United Nations force to influence its outcome, which is formally prohibited by the very paragraph which you invoked.

It is incomprehensible to me that you should have sent only Swedish and Irish troops to Katanga, systematically excluding troops from the African states even though some of the latter were the first to be landed at Leopoldville. In this matter you have acted in connivance with the rebel Government of Katanga and at the instigation of the Belgian Government.

In view of the foregoing, I submit to you the following requests:

1. To entrust the task of guarding all the airfields of the Republic to troops of the National Army and the Congolese police in place of United Nations troops.

2. To send immediately to Katanga Moroccan, Guinean, Ghanaian, Ethiopian, Mali, Tunisian, Sudanese, Liberian and Congolese troops.

3. To put. aircraft at the disposal of the Government of the Republic for the transportation of Congolese troops and civilians engaged in restoring order throughout the country.

4. To proceed immediately to seize all arms and ammunition distributed by the Belgians in Katanga to the partisans of the rebel Government, whether Congolese or foreign, and to put at the disposal of the Government of the Republic the arms and ammunition so

seized, as they are the property of the Government.

5. To withdraw all non-African troops from Katanga immediately.

I hope that you will signify your agreement to the foregoing. If my Government does not receive satisfaction it will be obliged to take other steps. My Government takes this occasion to thank the Security Council for the resolutions it adopted, of which my Government and the Congolese people unanimously approve and which they would like to see applied directly and without delay.

P. LUMUMBA, Prime Minister

From a letter from Dag Hammarskjöld, U.N. Secretary-General, to the Prime Minister of the Republic of the Congo, August 15, 1960

Leopoldville

Sir,

I have received your letter of today's date. In it I find allegations against the Secretary-General as well as objections to the Secretary-General's interpretation of the resolutions with the implementation of which he has been entrusted. In your letter you also submit certain requests which appear to derive from a position contrary to my interpretation of the resolutions.

There is no reason for me to enter into a discussion here either of those unfounded and unjustified allegations or of the interpretation of the Security Council's resolutions. As far as the actions requested by you are concerned I shall naturally follow the instructions which the Council may find it necessary or useful to give me.

I have the honour to be, etc.

DAG HAMMARSKJÖLD

From a letter to Dag Hammarskjöld, U.N. Secretary-General, August 15, 1960

Leopoldville

The letter I addressed to you on August 14 on behalf of the Government of the Republic of the Congo contains no allegations against the Secretary-General of the United Nations but rather reveals facts, which should be made known to the Security Council and to the world at large. The Government of the Republic is well aware that the position you have adopted is in no sense that of the Security Council, in which it continues to have confidence. It is paradoxical that you decided to inform the Government of the Republic only after making arrangements with Mr. Tshombe and the Belgians surrounding him. Furthermore, you at no time considered it advisable to consult the Government of the Republic as the resolution of the Security Council recommended you to do. The Government considers that you refused to give it the military assistance it needs and for which it approached the United Nations. I should be grateful if you would inform me in clear terms whether you reject the specific proposals contained in my letter of August 14. In expectation of an immediate reply, I have the honour to be, etc.

P. LUMUMBA, Prime Minister

From a letter from the United Nations Secretary-General to the Prime Minister of the Republic of the Congo, August 15, 1960

Leopoldville

Sir,

I received your letter of August 15 in reply to my letter of the same date. I presume that your letters have been approved by the Council of Ministers and that you will inform the Council of Ministers of my replies. I have nothing to add to my reply to your first communication dated August 14 and received today at noon.

Your letter will be circulated to the Security Council immediately at my request. If the Council of Ministers takes no initiative which compels me to change my plans, or has no other specific proposal to make, I shall go to New York this evening in order to seek clarification of the attitude of the Security Council.

I have the honour to be, etc.

DAG HAMMARSKJÖLD

From a letter to **Dag Hammarskjöld, U.N. Secretary-General, August 15, 1960**

Leopoldville,

Sir,

I have just this moment received your letter of today's date in reply to the one I sent you an hour ago. Your letter does not reply at all to the specific questions or concrete proposals contained in my letters of August 14 and 15. There is nothing erroneous in my statements, as you maintain. It was because I publicly denounced, at a recent press conference, your manoeuvres in sending to Katanga only troops from Sweden-a country which is known by public opinion to have special affinities with the Belgian royal family-that you have suddenly decided to send African troops into that province.

If no member of the Security Council has taken the initiative to question the validity of your Memorandum and your plans of action it is because the members of the Council do not know exactly what is going on behind the *scenes*. Public *opinion* knows-and the members of the Security Council also know-that after the adoption of the last resolution you delayed your journey to the Congo for twenty-four hours solely in order to have talks with Mr. Pierre

Wigny, Belgian Minister of Foreign Affairs, administrator of mining companies in the *Congo and one of* those who plotted the secession of Katanga. Before leaving New York for the Congo, the Congolese delegation, led by Mr. Antoine Gizenga, Vice-President of the Council of Ministers urgently requested you to contact my Government immediately upon your arrival in Leopoldville and before going to Katanga-which was in conformity with the Security Council's resolution of July14, 1960. I personally laid particular stress on this point in the letter I sent to you on August 12 through the intermediary of Mr. Ralph Bunche, your special representative.

Completely ignoring the legal Government of the Republic, you sent a telegram from New York to Mr. Tshombe, leader of the Katanga rebellion and emissary of the Belgian Government. Mr. Tshombe, again at the instigation of the Belgians placed at his side, replied to this telegram stipulating two conditions for the entry of United Nations troops into Katanga. According to the revelations just made by Mr. Tshombe at his press conference, you entirely acquiesced in the demands formulated by the Belgians speaking through Mr. Tshombe.

In view of all the foregoing, the Government and people of the Congo have lost their confidence in the Secretary-General of the

United Nations. Accordingly, we request the Security Council today to send immediately to the Congo a group of observers representing the following countries: Morocco, Tunisia, Ethiopia, Ghana, Guinea, the United Arab Republic, the Sudan, Ceylon, Liberia, Mali, Burma, India, Afghanistan and the Lebanon. The task of these observers will be to ensure the immediate and entire application of the Security Council resolutions of July 14 and 22 and August 9. I earnestly hope that the Security Council, in which we place our full confidence, will grant our legitimate request. A delegation of the Government will accompany you in order to express its views to the Security Council. I would, therefore, ask you kindly to delay your departure for twenty-four hours in order to permit our delegation to travel on the same aircraft.

P. LUMUMBA, Prime Minister

From a letter from the U.N. Secretary-General to the Prime Minister of the Congo, August 15, 1960

Sir,

Your third letter of today's date has just been received. I have taken note of your intention to send a delegation to the Security Council to request the dispatch of a group of observers to ensure the implementation of the Council's resolutions. This request would seem to be based on the statement which you have made that you no longer have confidence in me.

I shall not discuss your repeated erroneous allegations or the new allegations added to those which you have already addressed to me. It is for the Security Council to judge their worth and to assess the confidence which the member countries have in the Secretary-General of the United Nations. As regards the questions asked in your letters, to which you say you have had no reply, I refer you to the explanatory memorandum transmitted to you by Mr. Bunche. In it you will find all the necessary information.

You have requested me to delay my departure in order to enable the delegation of the Congo to travel on the same aircraft with me. I do not see the advantage of that arrangement, since it goes without saying that the Council will not meet until after the arrival of your delegation. In these circumstances, and as I have made all the preparations for my departure, I shall leave as indicated to you in an earlier letter today.

DAG HAMMARSKJÖLD

Source: 1. *letter: Patrice Lumumba, The Truth about a Monstrous Crime of the Colonialists, Moscow, Foreign Languages Publishing*

House, 1961, p. 71, the rest: **Patrice Lumumba: Fighter for Africa's Freedom**, *Moscow, Progress*

From a letter to the President of the Security Council

Patrice Lumumba, August 1, 1960

The trend of events in the Congo is causing my Government serious concern.....

The Belgian Government promised to withdraw its troops from the Congo as soon as the United Nations troops reached there.

United Nations troops have been arriving in the Congo since July 16, but not a single Belgian soldier has left Congolese soil.

We are at present confronted with a deliberate refusal by the Belgian Government to comply with the decisions of the highest international authority, the Security Council.

The Vice-Chairman of the Council of Ministers of the Republic of the Congo informs me in a telegram recently received in New York, a copy of which is attached, that the Congolese soldiers are being disarmed, whereas the Belgian soldiers are remaining in the territory together with all their arms. I would particularly draw your attention to the fact that no contingent of United Nations troops has so far entered Katanga, because this is opposed by the Belgian Government solely in order to strengthen the secession movement it has instigated in this province using Tshombe as a screen, in contravention of the relevant resolutions adopted by the Security Council.

There is now no justification whatever for the presence of Belgian military forces in the Congo.

The arguments put forward by the Belgian Government for the maintenance of its troops in the Congo contrary to the decisions of the Security Council are merely false pretexts. The Belgian Government's intention is to disorganise the country and involve our Government and our people in numerous economic and financial difficulties.

To give just one example, the Belgian Government recently removed our gold reserves which were in our Central Bank in the Congo. Such measures of economic strangulation are taking place in many other sectors.

I would also inform you that the people of Katanga emphatically repudiate the attempts at secession, which the Belgian Government is in the process of organising in that province with the help of a number of collaborators, among whom is Mr. Tshombe. The present objective of the Belgian Government and of a few groups which support it, is to bring about the division of the Congo in orderto obtain a hold over our country. The paramount problem in the Congo is that of the immediate withdrawal of all Belgian troops from Congolese territory.

I reserve the right to request a meeting of the Security Council to consider whatever measures may prove necessary.

P. LUMUMBA, Prime Minister

Source: Patrice Lumumba: Fighter for Africa's Freedom, *Moscow, Progress Publishers, 1961, pp 46-8..* **Written:** *by Patrice Lumumba;* **Transcribed:** *by Thomas Schmidt.*

From a telegram to the President of the Security Council

Patrice Lumumba, August 1, 1960

It has come to my knowledge that resorting to insidious manoeuvres and using Tshombe as its instrument, the Belgian Government is taking recourse to blackmail in order to prevent the arrival of United Nations troops in Katanga. All of Tshombe's actions are dictated by Belgian officers, whom the Belgian Government has placed at his side as advisers.

Clearly, the Belgian Government is torpedoing the fulfilment of the decisions of the United Nations.... The Security Council has virtually authorised you to take, in consultation with the Government of the Republic of the Congo, the necessary steps in order to provide us with whatever military assistance we may need.

With the purpose of keeping its troops in Katanga and thereby consolidating the secession of Katanga, which it instigated, the Belgian Government alleges that these troops were sent into Katanga at Tshombe's request. With this statement the Belgian Government admits that it instigated the secession of Katanga.

By placing its troops and military advisers at Tshombe's disposal in order to facilitate the splitting up of the Congo and hinder the actions of the United Nations, the BelgianGovernment is obviously opposing the restoration of legality and order in the Congo and the exercise of authority by the Government of the Congo.

I reaffirm my demand to you that United Nations troops be sent into Katanga immediately. Any delay in the strict fulfilment of the Security Council's decisions may seriously affect the prestige of the United Nations, as well as the security of the Congo, which will be a threat to peace in Africa. In the event United Nations troops are not brought into Katanga by Saturday, August 6, in conformity with the obligations undertaken by the United Nations, by you and by my Government, I shall be compelled to re-examine my position. I continue to hope....

P. LUMUMBA

Source: Patrice Lumumba: Fighter for Africa's Freedom, *Moscow, Progress Publishers, 1961, p 48f.* **Written:** *by Patrice Lumumba;* **Transcribed:** *by Thomas Schmidt.*

From the letter to the President of the UN General Assembly
Patrice Lumumba, November 11, 1960

The continuing political crisis provoked by the head of state, Mr. Kasavubu, on September 5, 1960 makes imminent the grave danger of the Congo's complete break-up. A regime of anarchy and dictatorship has replaced the democratic regime established by the Congolese people on June 30, 1960. A tiny minority, advised and financed by certain foreign powers, is engaged in subversive activity night and day. The capital of the republic is a scene of disorder, where a handful of hired military men are ceaselessly violating law and order. The citizens of Leopoldville now live under a reign of terror. Arbitrary arrests, followed by deportation, arc a daily and nightly occurrence, and many persons are reported missing. Murder, burglary and rape of married women and young girls are committed almost daily by individuals bereft of every sense of morality and patriotism, who profess to be in the service of the national army and of Mr. Kasavubu.

The presidents of the provincial governments of Stanleyville and Leopoldville, Mr. Finant and Mr. Kamitatu, recognised leaders, elected by the people, and governing between them more than six million inhabitants to the satisfaction of all concerned, are at this moment subjected to every conceivable form of brutality and torture. These two provincial presidents-men wholly dedicated to the task of improving the well-being of their people-were taken by surprise by Mobutu's thugs respectively on October 13, 1960 at Stanleyville and November 10 at Leopoldville and are now in concentration camps set up at Leopoldville by Messrs. Kasavubu and Mobutu.

The only fault of these worthy representatives of the people is loyalty to their country and disapproval of the unlawful acts of Mr. Kasavubu and his followers at Leopoldville, acts which are leading the country straight to disaster.

Mr. Joseph Okito, President of the Senate, the second highest dignitary in the state, has had the same experience. He has several times been arbitrarily arrested, beaten and then set free. Similar crimes are daily committed against the members of the majority group in Parliament and the members of the legally constituted government. They have even been officially prohibited to leave Leopoldville and return to their provinces to meet their constituents and join their families; they are restricted in their movements in Leopoldville, which after all belongs to the entire nation. At Leopoldville the majority parties in Parliament are forbidden to publish newspapers.

All loyal army personnel and government officials, who wanted to have no truck with the unlawful activities and the policy of national demolition pursued by the head of state and his handful of supporters at Leopoldville, have been dismissed from their posts, maltreated and turned out into the street. Hundreds of loyal soldiers who oppose Mobutu are sent back daily to their villages; others are now in the Binza concentration camp. Soldiers are recruited on the basis of ethnic kinship with the head of state and his minority supporters, the purpose being to terrorise those who do not share their views and opinions. Those who honestly and loyally champion the cause of the people are now being butchered. The provisional institutions envisaged under the Fundamental Law drawn up by the former colonial power have been undermined and trampled in the dust by the head of state.

Because it does not agree with him, Parliament has been high-handedly dismissed in violation of Articles 21 and 70 of the Fundamental Law. Mr. Kasavubu confuses the parliamentary regime, which is our system, with the presidential regime. That is why he assumes the powers vested in the Prime Minister under Article 36 of the Fundamental Law. It is not for the head of state but for the Prime Minister and my lawful government to send delegations to the United Nations, as I have done on three occasions. Parliament, the country's supreme organ, voted full powers to my government on September 13, 1960. The confidence placed in my government by the entire nation is steadily increasing. The United Nations is not entitled to choose any course other than the one indicated by Parliament. Certain slates, which are members of the United Nations, instead of conforming to the decisions taken by the sovereign Congolese Parliament, ignore them and support only the minority working against the will of the majority.

Instead of helping the Congolese leaders to effect a peaceful settlement of the conflict provoked by Mr. Kasavubu, certain powers are doing their utmost to widen the breach between us, their plan being indirectly to bring about the dismemberment of the Congo. In this connection, the Congolese people as a whole deplore the attitude of the United States Government; it is with great regret that I call the General Assembly's attention to the fact that, as eloquently testified by the documents seized, the 30 million francs recently confiscated at Stanleyville from a group of persons plotting to seize power by a *coup d'etat* came from United States sources. In view of the foregoing, and of the fact that the United Nations has proved unable to find a prompt solution in accordance with the expressed will of the people, I propose, with the backing of the millions of inhabitants I lawfully represent, that the solution of the

Congolese problem should be left to the Congolese people themselves.

No one will then be able to accuse the United Nations of partiality in any eventual decision, or of interference in the Congo's internal affairs. With this end in view, I propose that a popular referendum be held without delay with the participation of all the citizens of the republic, under the direction of the provincial assemblies and governments but under the supervision of a commission of United Nations observers. The said commission would do everything to ensure that all electors cast their votes freely. Steps would also be taken to prevent any fraud.

The referendum would relate to the adoption of a presidential regime, to be followed by the election of the President of the Republic by direct suffrage. Such a referendum would enable the people to choose freely and directly the leaders they want and thus to put an end to the present crisis and to all the backstage manoeuvring. This is the one and only way of restoring immediate peace and order in the Congo and so serving the interests of the mission undertaken by the United Nations in our country.

Please accept, Mr. President, assurances of my high esteem.

P. E. LUMUMBA

Solemn Appeal to the President and members of the Security Council and to all the member states of the United Nations
Patrice Lumumba, September 10, 1960

In a Memorandum dated September 8, 1960, and addressed to the Secretary-General of the United Nations and the President of the Security Council, the Government of the Republic of the Congo drew attention to the United Nations' flagrant interference in the internal affairs of the Congo. Conclusive proof was given of this interference. The statement just made in the Security Council by the U.N. Secretary-General that Mr. Kasavubu had the right to depose the Government only confirms this interference.

Moreover, the position adopted by the Secretary-General runs counter to the sovereign decisions of the Congolese Parliament, which in two ballots, with a considerable majority of votes in each ballot, annulled the decree illegally issued by Mr. Kasavubu.

It is not the U.N. Secretary-General's business to interpret the Fundamental Law of the land; that is the duty of the Congolese Parliament. Article 51 states that the "formal interpretation of laws is the exclusive responsibility of the Chambers". In their interpretation, in particular, of Article 22, according to which the "Head of State appoints and deposes the Prime Minister and Ministers", the two Chambers of the Congolese Parliament, which annulled the decree of the Head of State, came to the conclusion that a government can be appointed or deposed only after Parliament has passed a vote of confidence or no confidence.

The Head of State cannot appoint a government without the sanction of Parliament and that, to an equal degree, applies to the deposition of a government, which must follow the same procedure. Furthermore, in their interpretation, the Congolese legislative Chambers declared that insofar as the Government, headed by Prime Minister Patrice Lumumba, and the Head of State Mr. Kasavubu, had been approved separately by Parliament, only the latter had the right to depose the one or the other.

Basing itself on the confidence unanimously expressed in the Government by Parliament, which is the only sovereign body in the country, the Government of the Republic lodges a further protest against the interference of Secretary-General Hammarskjöld in the internal affairs of the Congolese nation. This interference is a grave threat to confidence in the United Nations and its prestige not only in the Congo but also throughout Africa and, essentially, throughout the world. In addition, the Government of the Republic lodges a further protest against the repeated refusal of the United Nations authorities in the Congo to co-operate with the Government in implementing the Security Council's resolutions. In the interests of universal peace, the Government urgently requests the United Nations:

1. Firmly to recommend to the Secretary-General and his colleagues in the Congo that they should cease interfering in the internal affairs of our Republic directly or indirectly.

2. Not to adopt any further resolutions on the Congo insofar as the resolutions already adopted are perfectly clear and specific but have not been fully implemented because of the perfidy of the Belgian Government and its allies, who are continuing to help the illegal and rebel Government of Katanga with supplies of aircraft, arms and ammunition and with liaison and line officers.

To this is added the fact that the United Nations authorities are deliberately holding up the implementation of the concrete and unequivocal decisions of the Security Council.

The Congolese Government cannot be deceived by these intrigues, which are turning the dispute between the Congo and Belgium into a dispute between the Government of the Congo and the United Nations only ten days after our Republic formally became a member of the U.N.

The Government most emphatically protests against the contention of the Secretary-General that troops of the National Army must be disarmed. Being perfectly aware that the troops of the National Army did not submit to a similar demand by Mr. Kasavubu, who ordered the Congolese militia to lay down their arms, the Secretary-General would like to continue with a demonstration of force only in order to start a war in the Congo in which the Congolese population would find itself in conflict with the armed forces of the United Nations.

The sole purpose of all this is to establish an international trusteeship over the Congo. Moreover, by such arbitrary actions as the seizure of our national radio station and all the airfields in the Republic, the Secretary-General seeks to deprive the Government of the means of broadcasting and to prevent any outflow of information in order to allow Tshombe and the illegal radio stations that have been recently set up near Leopoldville to continue their attempts at a coup d'etat. These stations are daily spreading active anti-Government propaganda, lies, slander and insults in order to discredit the legal Government, which has the support of the overwhelming majority of the people.

This morning the Government informed the U.N. Headquarters for the fifth time that it must regain the use of its national radio station. Anxious to restore peace and order in the Congo and to retain good relations with the United Nations, the Government of the Republic of the Congo solemnly and passionately appeals to all the countries of the world to take steps to prevent the Congo from being turned into a battlefield of a third world war.

P. LUMUMBA

Source: Patrice Lumumba: Fighter for Africa's Freedom, *Moscow, Progress Publishers, 1961, pp. 67-70.* **Written:** *by Patrice Lumumba;* **Transcribed:** *by Thomas Schmidt.*

Statement at a press conference in Leopoldville
Patrice Lumumba, August 16, 1960

I have asked you to this press conference primarily to announce to you an important decision that the present situation has forced the Government of the Republic to take.

You shall see that we are conscious of the gravity of the hour and are not shirking our responsibilities. The reason for calling this conference is that I wanted to determine the present situation with you.

Yesterday, from the U.N. services, you received a version of the divergences between the U.N. Secretary-General and our Government. Some people are seeking to present this dispute as a question of personality, of personalities. I should like to emphasise here and now that the U.N. Secretary-General is a high officer in the service of an institution that we respect to the point that we have appealed to it (for aid-*Tr.*). However, here the question is to examine, on the basis of facts, the Secretary-General's mission and the manner in which he has or has not fulfilled this mission.

Everything was perfectly clear in the evening of July 14 in New York, when Security Council decided, I quote the text of the resolution, "to authorise the Secretary-General to take, in consultation with the Government of the Republic of the Congo, all necessary measures with a view to giving that Government the military assistance it requires until such a time when the national security forces, thanks to the efforts of the Congolese Government and with the technical assistance of the United Nations, are, in the opinion of that Government, fully capable of carrying out their tasks".

From this it is quite clear that the Secretary-General had no business giving his own interpretation of the order instructing him to extend to our Government unrestricted military assistance, which we required and still require and with regard to which we are the sole judges.

We asked the U.N. for assistance, and it responded to our appeal. Our attitude towards the United Nations remains one of full trust. Strong and confident of our right, we are profoundly convinced that the U.N., which has already demonstrated its insight and impartiality with regard to us, will straightforwardly carry out the decisions it has adopted.

Let me emphasise once again that the matter concerns the maintenance of peace among nations.

That is why we regret some of the actions that have been taken by the Secretary-General, and you are bearing witness that these actions are only prolonging the crisis, which we are the first to deplore.

Incidents, which U.N. troops should have stopped long ago, are taking place every day because of the behaviour of the aggressive Belgian forces and because of certain ambiguities created by some groups.

On the other hand, all the Belgian magistrates have fled, leaving their offices in indescribable disorder, with the result that civil courts no longer exist.

We have decided to take immediate steps to hold in check all trouble-makers, white or black, in order to enable our people to retrieve their dignity and to restore legality and peace.

I shall now read you the ordinance that was promulgated by the Government today.

[P. Lumumba reads the text of the ordinance.]

I shall now give you some figures to show that with goodwill each can make his contribution towards the solution of our problems.

In the period from August 1 to 8, the Matadi-Leopoldville Railway transported 6,000 tons of timber. During the past week this figure has been nearly trebled to 17,500 tons. In other words, in the past eight days we have restored the normal rhythm.

This encouraging result was achieved with only 5 per cent of the former European personnel. We greet the work that has been done by these people. The Government of the Republic takes this occasion to reaffirm the friendship of the Congolese population for the Belgian people. It confirms that it is ready to restore diplomatic relations with Belgium as soon as Belgian troops withdraw from the Congo, including the bases at Kitona and Kamina. We are prepared to renew friendly relations.

Source: Patrice Lumumba: Fighter for Africa's Freedom, *Moscow, Progress Publishers, 1961, pp 59-61.* **Written:** *by Patrice Lumumba;* **Transcribed:** *by Thomas Schmidt.*

Statement at a press conference in Leopoldville

Patrice Lumumba, August 17, 1960

At my yesterday's press conference I stated the grave reasons that prompted the Government to ask the President of the Security Council to examine the question of immediately sending a group of neutral observers to the Congo to ensure control over the implementation of the resolution of July 14, 1960. Certain circles with interests in the Congo have qualified our position as a lack of confidence in the U.N. As I stated yesterday and repeat again, the matter here is not in a lack of trust or in any suspicion with regard to the U.N. On the contrary, The Government and the people of the Congo continue to trust the U.N. and its Security Council. What we have condemned, and that can be proved, is only the method by which the U.N. Secretary-General sought to implement the Security Council's resolutions. He acted as though there were no Government of the Republic.

The Congolese people regard his contacts and meetings with Tshombe as well as the assurances that he gave Tshombe as treachery. Tshombe did not conceal the fact that he had official assurances from the U.N. Secretary-General. In conformity with the Security Council's resolutions, Mr.

Hammarskjöld should not have had talks with Tshombe. Furthermore, the Secretary-General did not once show any desire to consult with the Government of the Republic as he was officially advised to do by the resolution of July 14, 1960.

Consequently, a line must be drawn between the personal actions of Mr. Hammarskjöld, which we brand in the name of truth and justice, and the far-sighted policy of the United Nations. In the Congo nobody approves the steps that have so far been taken in the Congo issue by the U.N. Secretary-General. His interpretation of the Security Council's decisions clearly shows us his intentions. The Government is aware that certain circles seek to turn the Congo into a second Korea. And in order to achieve this purpose by roundabout ways, implementation of the decisions of an organ of the highest international authority is being delayed. Many crimes have been perpetrated in Katanga because of the U.N. Secretary-General's delay in carrying out the decisions of the United Nations.

The fact of the matter is that several scores of Congolese, military personnel and civilians, were shot two days ago. These repugnant crimes have been concealed from the public. Surely the U.N. Secretary-General knows about it. The conspiracy of silence designed to delude world public opinion is noteworthy. The

Belgian press and the correspondents sent to Katanga assert that order reigns there, whereas in reality arbitrary shootings and arrests are occurring every day as a consequence of Tshombe's compact with Belgium. Every day I receive disturbing news from various parts of Katanga and every day the people of Katanga Province are asking the Government to intervene and deliver them from the oppression of the Belgium-Tshombe group.

Conscience will not allow the Government to permit such a situation to continue in the country. We wanted to go to the Security Council to condemn this situation, for all to hear, believing that if our official delegation were absent the Security Council might be misinformed. I asked the U.N. Secretary-General to postpone his departure for 24 hours to enable our Government delegation to accompany him. Our request was turned down. And yet in his letter of August 15, 1960, he assured me that the Security Council would meet only after the arrival of our delegation. To my great surprise and to the surprise of the whole of Congolese public opinion, I learned that the Security Council is to meet tomorrow morning although the delegation of the Congo has not left the country because of transportation difficulties.

This morning I cabled the President of the Security Council, asking him to postpone the meeting until the arrival of a delegation from the Congolese Government.

I hope that this well-founded request is complied with. Moreover, I hope that the Government will not be compelled to renounce the services of the U.N. In the event a decision we shall consider as undesirable is taken, that is to say, if a group of neutral foreign observers will not be sent with instructions to ensure control over the implementation of the Security Council's resolutions, the Government will, to its regret, be forced to consider other, speedier measures. More than a month of our hopes in the U.N. and of waiting has passed. It is over a month now that we have been waiting for its resolutions to be carried out.

It does not do for any country to lecture us or to tell us what road we should take if there is no desire to help us in the way we have asked and if it is contemplated to use our request for military aid to pursue other political aims. We are prepared to withdraw this request. Nobody can enter the Congo and no foreign power can set foot in our country and interfere in its affairs if it has not been specifically requested to do so by the legal Government of the Congo Republic. The Congo is a sovereign, independent and free state with the same rights as France, Belgium, Britain and the U.S.A. We are the masters of our own destinies and we shall make the Congo into what we want her to be and not into what others want. Those who reproach me for telling the truth and exposing certain manoeuvres are giving themselves away in the face of this truth, because it will triumph in the very near future. Together with our people we shall defend our country to the end, regardless of the plots and manoeuvres of the Belgian colonialists and their allies. History will show who is right.

Patrice Lumumba

Source: Patrice Lumumba: Fighter for Africa's Freedom, Moscow, Progress Publishers, 1961, pp 61-64. **Written:** by Patrice Lumumba; **Transcribed:** by Thomas Schmidt.

Statement at a press conference

Patrice Lumumba, August 19, 1960

This morning Mr. Bunche handed me a note from the U.N. Secretary-General.

In it Mr. Hammarskjöld gives an account of a trivial incident between U.N. forces and the Congolese army. The Secretary-General and his representatives in Leopoldville have deliberately exaggerated this incident with the sole purpose of using it to further their aims on the eve of the Security Council meeting. Their purpose is to influence the opinion of the Security Council members in favour of the Secretary-General, who has compromised himself by his actions in Katanga. This manoeuvre must be publicly exposed.

What really happened is this. The Government of the Republic decreed a state of emergency throughout the country. On the other hand it was found that many foreigners are entering the Congo without the agreement of the Government of the Republic. For them the Congo has become an international market. These people are spying and continuously instigating disorders in the country.

In this situation it was decided to check the identity of all passengers of aircraft belonging to foreign powers. This check was conducted with every sign of courtesy.

Upon the arrival of two aircraft transporting Canadian military personnel, the security forces wished to check the identity of these passengers. But the latter flatly refused to produce their identification papers and hurled coarse language at the Congolese officials.

And even graver was the fact that Swedish troops of the U.N. force prevented the legal authorities from carrying out this check.

It was, first and foremost, this attitude of the passengers and then the behaviour of the European troops of the U.N. that started the incident.

Let me point out that every day troops of the National Army are attacked and unjustly insulted by U.N. European military personnel. The latter seek to take the place of the Government of the country and the legal authorities.

Moreover, some days ago I notified Mr. Bunche, the General-Secretary's special representative, of the Government's decision to have all the airfields in the Republic turned over to the exclusive control of troops of the National Army. The United Nations representatives refused to comply with this decision of the supreme authority of the Republic.

In view of this insolent attitude of the United Nations white troops sent into the Congo, the Government was compelled to demand their immediate withdrawal and allow only African troops to enter the Congo under U.N. control. This will enable us to avoid a cold war, because some states are now using units sent to the Congo from certain European countries to further their own interests. This has already been proved, and for the benefit of the Security Council I stress once again that the Government of the Republic has passed a decision on the withdrawal of all military units belonging to European nations.

We have stated, on the other hand, that the United Nations special representative in the Congo has distributed U.N. armbands among Belgian nationals and that they have used this badge to attack the Congolese population.

The U.N. Secretary-General declares in his note that he will be obliged to ask the Security Council to reconsider the entire United Nations action in the Congo. This blackmail by the Secretary-General does not surprise us.

To this my reply is that for its part the Government of the Republic is prepared to renounce the services of the United Nations, because the Congo, a sovereign and independent country, is nobody's property. We can easily and quickly restore order by ourselves and with the direct assistance that we can get from a number of countries, which have already given us their selfless support.

The Government of the Republic:

1. Condemns the personal actions of the U.N. Secretary-General;

2. Demands the immediate withdrawal of white troops, who were behind the latest incidents and who have shown bad intent with regard to the Republic;

3. Demands and repeats its request that a group of observers from neutral countries, a list of which has already been submitted to the Security Council, be sent to the Congo;

4. Confirms its desire loyally to co-operate with the United Nations in establishing peace on earth.

Patrice Lumumba concluded his statement by pointing out that it was only the intervention of some African states that forced the Secretary-General to give up his intention of placing the Congolese Government before an accomplished fact by convening the Security Council before the arrival of a Congolese delegation. He confirmed the trust of the Congolese Government in the United Nations and the Security Council. "We appealed for the services of the United Nations ourselves," he emphasised. "If some countries aspire to use the Secretary-General for their own purposes, we say to them that they will be condemned by the

African peoples." Lumumba pointed out that even if circumstances compelled the Congolese Government to renounce the services of the United Nations, it would not mean that the Congo would withdraw from that organisation because it did not identify the actions of individuals with the ideals of the United Nations.

Patrice Lumumba

Source: Patrice Lumumba: Fighter for Africa's Freedom,
Moscow, Progress Publishers, 1961, pp 64-7. **Written:** *by Patrice*
Lumumba;
Transcribed: *by Thomas Schmidt.*

Interview

Washington, July 28, 1960, TASS

Prime Minister Patrice Lumumba of the Congo, who is now in Washington, gave the following interview to a TASS correspondent.

Question: How, in your opinion, is the U.N. Security Council decision on the rapid withdrawal of Belgian troops from the Congo being fulfilled?

Answer: Belgium has already proved that she has no respect for Security Council decisions. The Belgian Government is continuing its aggressive actions and savage reprisals against our people. It will be recalled that as far back as July 14, the Security Council demanded in a resolution that Belgian troops should leave the Congo; it sent U.N. armed forces to our country to back up this decision. But since then not a single Belgian soldier has left the territory of the Congo. Every day the troops of the Belgian colonialists kill soldiers of our national army and massacre hundreds of Congolese civilians. These facts are not widely known in the world because the Belgian colonialists have got the press of other Western countries to write as little as possible about the doings of Belgian soldiers in the Congo.

Our government and Parliament have from the very first demanded that Belgian troops should leave the Congo. The pertinent Soviet proposal tabled in the Security Council was the only proposal fully conforming to our people's interests. We continue to demand and declare that the immediate withdrawal of Belgian troops is the only way of restoring law and order in the Congo. That is why we ask all democratic and peace-loving countries to support our demand. The last Belgian soldier should have left the Congo long ago. The U. N. troops, which arrived to ensure implementation of the Security Council's resolution, have now been in the Congo for over a fortnight. But the situation has not changed. I must say that the Security Council's resolutions are being fulfilled anything but properly, although the Council had already passed two resolutions—on July 14 and 22—on the need to withdraw Belgian troops from the Congo. Such a small country as Belgium allows herself to behave in this way only because the Congo now lacks the weapons to throw out the Belgian colonialists.

Question: What is the situation in Katanga? What is your opinion of Katanga's so-called secession from the Congo recently announced by Mr. Tshombe?

Answer: There has never been a Katanga problem as such. The gist of the matter is that the imperialists want to lay their hands on our country's riches and to continue exploiting our people. The imperialists have always had their agents in the colonial countries. Tshombe, in particular, is an agent of the Belgian imperialists. Everything he says and writes is not his own. He merely mouths the words of the Belgian colonialists. It is well known that Tshombe is an ex-businessman who has long since thrown in his lot with the colonial companies in the Congo. But very few people know that just recently, as a result of dishonest machinations and overdrafts, Tshombe owed Belgian companies in the Congo more than ten million Belgian francs. He was arrested and was to be tried. But in view of the situation that took shape, Tshombe was "pardoned" and released by the Belgians and since then he has been obediently carrying out all their orders.

Question: What is the Congolese people's view of the Soviet Union's stand on the Congo's struggle to attain genuine independence and territorial integrity?

Answer: The Soviet Union was the only Great Power whose stand conformed to our people's will and desire. That is why the Soviet Union was the only Great Power which has all along been supporting the Congolese people's struggle. I should like to convey the heartfelt gratitude of the entire Congolese people to the Soviet people and to Prime Minister Nikita Khrushchev personally for your country's timely and great moral support to the young Republic of the Congo in its struggle against the imperialists and colonialists. I should also like to thank the Soviet Union for the assistance in food which it is extending to the Congo.

Patrice Lumumba

Source: **Patrice Lumumba, The Truth about a Monstrous Crime of the Colonialists**, Moscow, Foreign Languages Publishing House, 1961, pp. 53-55. **Written**: by Patrice Lumumba; **Transcribed**: by Thomas Schmidt.

Letter to A.M. Dayal, Special Representative of the U.N. Secretary General

Thysville, January 4, 1961

Mr. Special Representative,

On December 27 last, I had the pleasure of receiving a visit from the Red Cross, which occupied itself with my plight and with the plight of the other parliamentarians imprisoned together with me. I told them of the inhuman conditions we are living in.

Briefly, the situation is as follows. I am here with seven other parliamentarians. In addition there are with us Mr. Okito, President of the Senate, a Senate employee and a driver. Altogether there are ten of us. We have been locked up in damp cells since December 2, 1960 and at no time have we been permitted to leave them. The meals that we are brought twice a day are very bad. For three or four days 1 ate nothing but a banana. I told this to the Red Cross medical officer sent to me. I spoke to him in the presence of a colonel from Thysville.

I demanded that fruit be bought on my own money because the food that I am given here is atrocious. Although the medical officer gave his permission, the military authorities guarding me turned down my request, stating that they were following orders from Kasavubu and Colonel Mobutu. The medical officer from Thysville prescribed a short walk every evening so that I could leave my cell for at least a little while. But the colonel and the district commissioner denied me this. The clothes that I wear have not been washed for thirty-five days. I am forbidden to wear shoes.

In a word, the conditions we are living in are absolutely intolerable and run counter to all rules.

Moreover, I receive no news of my wife and I do not even know where she is. Normally I should have had regular visits from her as is provided for by the prison regulations in force in the Congo. On the other hand, the prison regulations clearly state that not later than a day after his arrest a prisoner must be brought before the investigator handling his case. Five days after this a prisoner must again be arraigned before a judge, who must decide whether to remand him in custody or not. In any case, a prisoner must have a lawyer.

The criminal code provides that a prisoner is released from prison if five days after he is taken into custody the judge takes no decision on remanding him. The same happens in cases when the first decision (which is taken five days after a person is arrested) is not reaffirmed within fifteen days. Since our arrest on December 1 and to this day we have not been arraigned before a judge or visited by a judge. No arrest warrant has been shown to us. We are kept simply in a military camp and have been here for thirty-four days. We are kept in military detention cells.

The criminal code is ignored as are the prison rules. Ours is purely a case of arbitrary imprisonment. I must add that we possess parliamentary immunity. Such is the situation and I ask you to inform the United Nations Secretary-General of it. I remain calm and hope the United Nations will help us out of this situation. I stand for reconciliation between all the children of this country. I am writing this letter secretly on bad paper. I have the honour to be, etc.

Patrice LUMUMBA, Prime Minister

Radio Broadcast Message

Patrice Lumumba, September 5, 1960

The National Radio has just broadcast a declaration by the Head of State, Mr. Joseph Kasavubu, according to which the Government headed by me must be dismissed.

On behalf of the Government and the entire nation I formally reject this information.

The Government has had no talks on this subject with the Head of State. The Government, which has been democratically elected by the nation and has won the unanimous confidence of Parliament, can only be dismissed when it loses the trust of the people.

Today the Government enjoys this trust and has the backing of the entire people.

Having adopted the decision to defend the people at the price of blood, refused to sell the country to the Belgian colonialists and their allies, and frustrated the intrigues of those who still aim to exploit our nation, the Government will defend the rights of the people with honour and dignity.

The Government remains in power and shall continue fulfilling its mission.

I ask the population, which has vested us with trust, to be calm in the face of the manoeuvres of the saboteurs of our national independence.

We elected the Head of State ourselves even though he did not have the trust of the people. We can use the same right and withdraw this confidence if he goes against the interests of the people.

Congolese people, be vigilant. The enemies of our country and the accomplices of the Belgian imperialists are unmasking themselves.

Congolese officers and non-commissioned officers, remain at your posts in order to defend the country as heroically as when you fought against the Belgian aggressors.

Source: Patrice Lumumba: Fighter for Africa's Freedom,
Moscow, Progress Publishers, 1961, pp 37-38. **Written**: *by Patrice
Lumumba;*
Transcribed: *by Thomas Schmidt.*

Letter from Thysville Prison to Mrs. Lumumba

My dear,

I am writing these words to you, not knowing whether they will ever reach you, or whether I shall be alive when you read them.

Throughout my struggle for the independence of our country I have never doubted the victory of our sacred cause, to which I and my comrades have dedicated all our lives. But the only thing which we wanted for our country is the right to a worthy life, to dignity without pretence, to independence without restrictions.

This was never the desire of the Belgian colonialists and their Western allies, who received, direct or indirect, open or concealed, support from some highly placed officials of the United Nations, the body upon which we placed all our hope when we appealed to it for help.

They seduced some of our compatriots, bought others and did everything to distort the truth and smear our independence. What I can say is this—alive or dead, free or in jail—it is not a question of me personally.

The main thing is the Congo, our unhappy people, whose independence is being trampled upon. That is why they have shut us away in prison and why they keep us far away from the people. But my faith remains indestructible.

I know and feel deep in my heart that sooner or later my people will rid themselves of their internal and external enemies, that they will rise up as one in order to say 'No' to colonialism, to brazen, dying colonialism, in order to win their dignity in a clean land.

We are not alone. Africa, Asia, the free peoples and the peoples fighting for their freedom in all corners of the world will always be side by side with the millions of Congolese who will not give up the struggle while there is even one colonialist or colonialist mercenary in our country. To my sons, whom I am leaving and whom, perhaps, I shall not see again, I want to say that the future of the Congo is splendid and that I expect from them, as from every Congolese, the fulfilment of the sacred task of restoring our independence and our sovereignty.

Without dignity there is no freedom, without justice there is no dignity and without independence there are no free men. Cruelty, insults and torture can never force me to ask for mercy, because I prefer to die with head high, with indestructible faith and profound belief in the destiny of our country than to live in humility and renounce the principles which are sacred to me.

The day will come when history will speak. But it will not be the history which will be taught in Brussels, Paris, Washington or the United Nations. It will be the history which will be taught in the countries which have won freedom from colonialism and its puppets. Africa will write its own history and in both north and south it will be a history of glory and dignity.

Do not weep for me. I know that my tormented country will be able to defend its freedom and its independence.

Long live the Congo! Long live Africa!

Patrice LUMUMBA

Thysville prison

Source: Patrice Lumumba, The Truth about a Monstrous Crime of the Colonialists, Moscow, Foreign Languages Publishing House, 1961, pp. 230-231.

Written: by Patrice Lumumba; Transcribed: by Thomas Schmidt.

WRITINGS ABOUT

PATRICE LUMUMBA

BY OTHER AUTHORS

In the struggle for Independence

Henri LAURENT

His name appeared on the political horizon in the days when the rattle of tommy-guns was heard in Leopoldville and Stanleyville.

Baudouin I, King of Belgium, had arrived in the Congo. That was in December 1959. Lumumba, founder of the Congo National Movement Party, was in prison. The king, it was said, would establish concord between the whites and the Negroes. The royal triumphal voyage was announced as though white men had never shed the blood of Negroes, as though the Congolese would fall down on their faces at the sight of the white king and chant his praise for his benefactions. Inwardly, the colonialists felt jittery. They were wondering whether it would not be the other way round, whether the king would not be hooted. They started cleverly spreading rumours among the Congolese. It was whispered into their ears that Baudouin I was a "good white man", that he would have Patrice Lumumba released from prison into which the "bad white men" had thrown him.

They were obliged to release him only when the notorious round-table conference started in Brussels, at which the independence of the Congo was fixed for June 30, 1960.

Lumumba arrived at the conference with the marks of manacles on his wrists. Like the other Congolese leaders, he was an object of exaggerated attentions. Money was offered to him. Hypocritical expressions of regret at his ill-treatment were made to him.

Of course, Count Gobert d'Aspremont-Lynden, the Grand Maréchal of the Court of Baudouin I, was not at the conference in person. But his nephew, Count Harold d'Aspremont-Lynden, was. The interests of the first administrator of the Katanga Company were defended by the second. Now that nephew is a member of the Belgian Cabinet.

Minister Ganshof van der Meersch also addressed the conference. He pressed his hand to his heart and was profuse in his expressions of love for the Congolese. His son, a naturalised American citizen, arrived in Belgium at that time. He had come to Brussels to explore the ground in the interests of powerful financial corporations in the U.S.A. Others behind the scenes were Gillet and Cousin, President and General Director of the Union Miniere, Humble, President of l'Union des Colons of Katanga, who practically came out in support of Tshombe. Colonel Weber was there, too, the man who was replaced by the French Colonel Trinquier as head of Tshombe's legions, the legions of the Union Miniere.

Lumumba was hard at work organising his movement in view of the coming general elections in the Congo. The colonialists had done their best to create a host of petty tribal opposition groups against him. Being set on securing the election of a Congolese Parliament that would serve them faithfully; they went to work still more intensively to fan inter-tribal animosity. Already at that time they were keeping Tshombe in reserve.

Proclaim the "independence" of Katanga? Why, what for? Everything in good time! The thing was, first, to try to keep the Congo whole. So the colonialists put on winning smiles for Lumumba....

But when the elections were held, when Lumumba's Party won a sweeping victory, which made it impossible to create a parliamentary majority against him, they got the wind up and started to manoeuvre. Lumumba was to be in the Government but not as its head. The idea was to make him a political captive, to use his name and prevent him from pursuing his own policy. It was like trying to make an elephant play the role of a mouse!

When this plan failed the Union Minière people called in their reserves. They praised Tshombe to the skies. They proclaimed the "independence" of Katanga, from where they hoped to reconquer the whole of the Congo.

What happened next, everyone knows. The armed intervention by Belgium, the United Nations.... The Central Government of the Republic was hamstrung by Hammarskjöld. The soldiers of this Government were disarmed on the pretext that all bloodshed was to be avoided.... At the same time Tshombe armed his forces with impunity! In the end Lumumba was delivered over to him bound hand and foot.

The imperialists knew what victim to choose. They dealt a dastardly blow at the symbol of Congolese independence and liberty. But do they really believe that in destroying the symbol they will destroy the cause it stood for? Lumumba was the object of their blind hatred. Things reached a point during the general strike in Belgium where the reactionary newspapers frequently represented the most respected leaders of the workers, the most courageous fighters for the cause of the working class, as people who "emulate Lumumba"! Actually, this cry of hatred was an admission of glory.

Following the expressions of horror which the murder of Patrice Lumumba and his two associates has evoked in the Congo and throughout the world, I hear the stirring cry "Justice!" This cry has reached Belgium, where those who paid Lumumba's assassins and shed the blood of the workers during the strike are hiding in their rich salons. The blood of the Prime Minister of the Congo, the blood of the workers of Belgium—the circle is completed. Imperialism stands branded with the badge of infamy.

Source: Patrice Lumumba: Fighter for Africa's Freedom, *Moscow, Progress Publishers, 1961, pp 90-93.* **Written:** *by Henri LAURENT, Belgian journalist;* **Transcribed:** *by Thomas Schmidt.*

Patrice Lumumba's Second Life

Tomas KOLESNICHENKO

This man has two lives. The first was cut short by the colonialists. The second will last eternally. Patrice Emery Lumumba, a young African with attentive, radiant eyes, has for ever taken his place in the ranks of heroic fighters who sacrificed their lives for human happiness. In the Congo we clearly saw this second life of the country's first Prime Minister, who chose torture and death rather than submit.

He has remained eternally young, fighting and unconquerable. Time has not yet stilled the pain. It seems only recently that he lived, laughed and frowned. "He made a speech at this very aerodrome," we were told by Albert Busheri, commissioner of Paulice in Orientale Province, whom we met in the spring of 1961. "The heat was unbearable, but the people stood absolutely still while Patrice spoke."

"What did he say?"

"I don't remember the words, but I can still hear his wrathful voice accusing the Belgian colonialists of crimes, of the infinite suffering they caused our country. Then a note of excitement crept in when he spoke of what our country would be like when it became independent. As I listened to him, I pictured a new Congo to myself, a Congo with factories, new houses, schools, hospitals, and new people—doctors and engineers—not Belgians but Congolese. There's nothing of that now."

A sad look appeared on Busheri's face. After a moment's silence he went on:

"We have a fine hospital here in Paulice, but it's not operating. There's not a single doctor in the town. But in spite of everything this country will be what Lumumba wanted it to be. You'll see...."

One evening we learned that in Paulice there was a man who was called Lumumba's teacher. It was already night when we knocked on the door of a small house on the outskirts of the town.

... Paul Kimbala was an elderly man. Our guides respectfully called him "father". He rose heavily to his feet, went to another room and came back with a tattered book. On it its owner had written in his own hand: "Patrice Lumumba". We carefully turned over the yellowed pages. A volume of lectures on logic, it had belonged to Lumumba. "I'm going to turn it over to a museum. We'll have Lumumba museums one day, and towns will be named after him," Kimbala said.

"Like Lumumba, I am a Batetela. We come from the same village. I knew his father well. His father was a Catholic and Patrice went to a Protestant school. Mission schools were the only places in the Congo where one could get an education. But he did not stay in that school long. Religion did not interest him and he was expelled. Later he came to live with me in Stanleyville. He worked and continued with his studies. He was an amazing youth. There was a library near our house and he used to spend every free moment in it. Every evening, I remember, he used to come home with a large heap of paper, which was covered with writing. 'They're extracts, father,' he said to me. 'They'll be useful to me.' I don't remember seeing him resting or simply making merry. Even when others would be singing and dancing or feasting, I would always see him with a book. Patrice was very persevering.

"Then he went to Leopoldville, where he studied in a Post Office school for six months. After he finished the school he wrote to me asking whether he should stay on in Leopoldville or return to Stanleyville. I advised him to return. He came back to Stanleyville and worked as the manager of a small Post Office branch 80 kilometres away from the town. All that time he regarded my home as his own. He married Pauline Opanga in my house. How happy he was at his wedding.

"In 1954 I moved to Paulice, leaving my house to Lumumba. I did not see him again until 1960."

Kimbala grew thoughtful. The flame flickered in the kerosene lamp on the small table. We sat with bated breath and the prolonged shrill notes of the cicadas were all that disturbed the silence of the Congolese night.

"The last time I saw Patrice," Kimbala said, resuming his story, "was in the summer of 1960, when he was the Prime Minister of the country. I visited him in Leopoldville. There were many people around him and it was impossible to get close to him. But I stood in the house and waited. Suddenly he saw me and came striding over to me. 'You came, father,' he said to me in our native Batetela. I had no money and asked him to help me. With an embarrassed smile he said: 'I don't have any money either, but we'll soon fix that.' He turned to the people around him and said: 'Who can give me some money?' Scores of hands were stretched out to him. It was our last meeting. I never saw- him again.

"Patrice was my pupil and I'm proud of him. I watched him begin his struggle. It was when he was working in a Post Office near Stanleyville. He and his friends frequently gathered in my house."

... In Stanleyville we did not have to look long for Patrice Lumumba's house. Everybody knew it, and people from all over the Congo came specially to see it. There were many people near the house when we arrived. They carried portraits of Lumumba and stood in silence. And on a green lawn, in front of the verandah where Pauline Lumumba and her younger son Roland were sitting, a group of peasants dressed in ancient national costumes were performing funeral dances to the beat of a tom-tom. The dancers swayed slowly in time to the rhythm. The tiny bells sewn on their costumes jingled, forming a contrast to the hollow sounds of the tom-tom.

The rhythm grew faster and soon the group was performing a war dance. The grief and hopeless despair in the beat of the tom-tom gave way to a call for vengeance.... Lumumba's family has a heavy burden of sorrow, but they are not alone. The people of the Congo remember their national hero. Darkness descends swiftly on the equator. When we left Lumumba's house, the lilac sky was covered with a black, star-spangled blanket. People were still standing near the house, and it seemed that the tall, thin man with the proud name of Patrice Emery Lumumba, who is living on, would appear at any moment.

*Source: **Patrice Lumumba: Fighter for Africa's Freedom**, Moscow, Progress Publishers, 1961, pp 110-113. **Written:** by Tomas KOLESNICHENKO, Soviet journalist; **Transcribed:** by Thomas Schmidt.*

The Congo before and after the arrest of the Prime Minister

(From the diary of Oleg ORESTOV, "Pravda" correspondent)

LEOPOLDVILLE, August 5

Yesterday the Council of Ministers of the Congo passed a decision on the expulsion from the country of the former Belgian Ambassador Van den Bosch. He was ordered to leave the country not later than Monday. Minister of Information Kashamura explained to correspondents that diplomatic relations with Belgium had been severed when the Belgians started their aggression against the Congo, but the Ambassador had illegally remained in the country.

Kashamura added that the former Ambassador was carrying on his political activity and making statements that were damaging the interests of the Congo, and the Council of Ministers had, therefore, been compelled to take resolute measures.

On the day before his expulsion Bosch called the Belgian correspondents together and told them that the relations between the Congo and Belgium were governed by an agreement signed on the eve of the Congo's independence and that this agreement could not be annulled unilaterally. The former Ambassador forgot to add that an event like Belgium's armed aggression against the Congo had taken place after the agreement had been signed and that as a result the relations between the two countries could not remain normal. Commenting on this illegal press conference, the newspaper *Congo* wrote: "The Government decided to close the Belgian Embassy, but the latter is openly laughing at this decision. The Belgian diplomat has the effrontery to assert that the Minister of Foreign Affairs of the Congo asked him to remain at his disposal." The newspaper added: "The former Belgian Ambassador is scoffing at our independence."

LEOPOLDVILLE, August 25

Public opinion in the Congo is continuing to demand that Belgian aggression should be stopped immediately. In a conversation with a group of correspondents, Prime Minister Lumumba declared that the Security Council had condemned the Belgian intervention in the Congo and that he hoped the Secretary-General would fulfil his commitment to clear the country of all Belgian troops within eight days.

Lumumba further stated that he protests against the attempt to leave "technical specialists" in the Congo because that was a mask for Belgian military personnel. He showed the note of protest that had just been sent to R.

Bunche, the U.N. Secretary-General's special representative in the Congo. In this document Lumumba pointed to a report in the Belgian newspaper *La libre Belgique,* which stated that 20 Belgian gendarmes were to be sent to Elisabethville as "technical aid to Katanga". Lumumba was surprised that Belgian gendarmes were being sent to the country as "technical aid" on the eve of the withdrawal of Belgian troops from Katanga and the dismantling of military bases there. He demanded that the U.N. should forbid their departure for the Congo as that would be a violation of the Security Council's resolution.

Some days ago Belgian military personnel arrived in the port of Matadi and high-handedly announced they had come for the military vehicles they had left behind. They were at once arrested by the Congolese police. Speaking of this incident to correspondents, a U.N. representative was forced to admit that there was an "understanding" between the Belgians and R. Bunche under which the Belgian military were allowed to return to the Congo for their "property". The U.N. representative claimed that Bunche had not had time to notify the Congolese authorities.

In Leopoldville yesterday the police arrested seven armed Belgians and turned them over to the security forces. These men were employees of the Sabena Airlines and had been making for the border. Today the police discovered three Belgians operating an illegal radio transmitter in a house in the heart of the city. Weapons were found in the house. The arrival of a large contingent of police saved the spies from the angry crowds of Congolese. The colonialists are aiding and abetting each other. A French aircraft has just landed in Kasai Province with emissaries of the traitor Tshombe and Belgian agents who plan to distribute arms to the local tribes and foment fresh disorders.

In reply to our questions Lumumba said that the Secretary-General has denied military assistance to the Republic of the Congo, and the Congolese people have decided to take action and restore order in the country themselves. Large contingents of the Congolese Army had already been dispatched to Kasai Province, where an armed clash inspired by agents of the imperialists had broken out between the tribes. "Our government," Lumumba said, "is morally bound to protect the population of Katanga Province even if the U.N. considers that its forces cannot 'interfere' in the matter. We are confident that we shall have the full backing of Katanga's population, which is whole-heartedly supporting the Central Government." The Prime Minister added that the puppet Tshombe regime would collapse as soon as Belgian troops would leave the military bases and Katanga Province.

ACCRA, December 6

All the newspapers are carrying alarming reports that Lumumba, who was seriously wounded by Mobutu's bandits, is being held in unbearable conditions in a military camp in Thysville. Reports from the Congo state that Mobutu's brigands had shaved his head and were keeping him imprisoned with his hands tied despite his serious wounds.

This time, too, U.N. representatives did nothing to save Lumumba. After arresting Lumumba, the self-appointed Colonel Mobutu became more arrogant than ever. Backed by the U.S.A., Belgium and other Western Powers, he now says that he will hold power indefinitely. He told a foreign correspondent that "as a political leader Lumumba is now finished". Mobutu's gangs are continuing their rampage. They attacked the town of Kikwit, where they disarmed the police and butchered the people. Twelve people were killed, more than 30 wounded and the rest of the population fled to the forests.

Mobutu's brazenness is imitated by his supporters under the traitor Kalondji in Kasai Province. Kalondji told Mobutu that he could transfer Lumumba to a jail in Bakwanga, which is controlled by Kalondji's gangs, saying that there he would be out of the reach of the U.N. forces. At the same time Kalondji demanded the arrest of Mkenji, the Prime Minister of the province, for speaking openly against the outrages committed by Mobutu's bandits.

Mobutu and his clique are worried by the news from Orientale Province and its capital, Stanleyville, where the national and genuinely democratic elements are especially strong. According to reports, Stanleyville stood firm against the dictates of Mobutu and the imperialists and was gathering forces to fight for complete independence. Frightened by this news, Mobutu made the delirious statement that if the U.A.R. and the Sudan support the national forces in Stanleyville he will "block the channels of the Nile's tributaries". The lunatic "colonel" announced: "In the last resort I will turn my army into an army of navvies and stop the water from flowing in the Nile."

ACCRA, December 8

According to people coming to Ghana from Leopoldville, the Congolese capital has been turned into an inferno. Today your correspondent interviewed E. Muenge who was in the Congo with a Ghanian technical aid team and has just returned to Accra. Asked what the situation was like in Leopoldville now, he said:

"After the Soviet Embassy and the representatives of the socialist countries left the Congo, Mobutu began his campaign against the independent African countries. By that time he had closed all the national progressive newspapers. Only two newspapers are being published and they are run by the Catholic priests and obvious Belgian stooges. This 'press' has launched a vile campaign against Ghana, Guinea, the U.A.R., Morocco and India. A Mobutu 'security officer' came to Welbeck, the Ghanian diplomatic representative, and handed him an 'order' to remove the Ghanian Embassy from the Congo. We were astonished to see that this order had been signed by President Kasavubu earlier. He was in New York when the incident occurred.

This confirmed that Kasavubu had acted jointly with Mobutu and had prepared the ground so that during the attack on the Ghanian Embassy he would not be in the Congo and would be able to deny that he bore any responsibility. On November 21, Mobutu sent lorries filled with troops to the residence of the Ghanian Ambassador. Tunisian units of the U.N. force also arrived on the scene and when 'Colonel' Kokolo, Mobutu's right-hand man, tried to enter the house they stopped him. When that happened Mobutu's soldiers opened fire on the Tunisians. Kokolo made an attempt to get into the house through a window and was shot dead by U.N. soldiers. The firing lasted all evening and night until dawn.

Nathaniel Welbeck left the Congo after receiving instructions to do so from his government. It is characteristic that the U.N. leaders did nothing to protect even the Leopoldville aerodrome against Mobutu's gangs. Some time ago they prevented representatives of Lumumba's Government from entering the aerodrome and even threatened to open fire if Lumumba officers appeared there. But now they calmly stand by and watch Mobutu's men lording it in the aerodrome, threatening the pilots of incoming aircraft, searching the aircraft and laying down the law as to which aircraft 'can' land in Leopoldville and which 'cannot'. After the departure of the Ghanian Embassy a similar campaign was started against the Embassy of the U.A.R. Attacks are planned against the embassies of other African countries, Guinea and Morocco in particular."

*Source: **Patrice Lumumba, The Truth about a Monstrous Crime of the Colonialists**, Moscow, Foreign Languages Publishing House, 1961, pp. 99-105. **Written:** by Oleg ORESTOV; **Transcribed:** by Thomas Schmidt.*

Last days of Freedom

Lev VOLODIN

The rain poured all that evening, and from our verandah we gazed at the turbid curtain of water that hid the silent city from view. Our host was 25-year-old Jacques N. With the quick gestures of a youth and the firm gaze of a man who had seen much in his life, he spoke in an emotion-filled voice of the days when Patrice Lumumba struggled against the men who accomplished the September coup d'etat. Jacques had been one of Lumumba's associates and had worked with him.

He told me how Lumumba's departure from his closely guarded residence was planned and carried out in November 1960. Jacques had helped in that daring escape and remembered everything down to the last detail. All I had to do was to write down what he said, to keep pace with his rapid flow of words. Here is his story:

It was a rainy evening. We were in Leopoldville, where we were surrounded by enemies. Lumumba had spent two months behind a double ring of troops. It was impossible to see him, but we spoke to him from time to time, using the telephone in a U.N. guardhouse.

On the first day of his imprisonment Lumumba ordered us to be prepared to leave

Leopoldville so as to continue an open fight against the rebels from some other place. Many political leaders, Ministers and M.P.s prepared to leave the city. According to Lumumba's plan the whole operation was to take one or two days and we were to go at different times and use different routes.

November 27, 1960, was the day set for our departure. All that day we waited for a telephone call from Lumumba. The telephone rang at six in the evening when an autumn tropical shower was pouring down from the sky.

"I am ready," Lumumba said. "Drive to the house and wait there."

Victor B. and I put two old rifles in our car and sped to Lumumba's house in the driving rain. Troops were patrolling the entrance. Most of them were hiding from the rain under a tree. We took in the entire scene at a glance. Our plan was simple: if the troops noticed Lumumba in the car we would fire at them to cover his escape.

The gates swung open and a big black Chevrolet appeared. The driver, Maurice, stopped the car and, replying to a query from the soldiers, said:

"I'm taking the servants home. It will soon be night."

In the rain and darkness the sergeant could not see who was in the car.

"Open the door, we'll check," he ordered the driver.

We released the safety catches on our rifles. The guards had only one rifle. The others were stacked beneath an awning. But at that moment we heard Lumumba cry:

"Maurice, step on the gas!"

The powerful car sprang forward; the soldiers shouted and ran for their rifles. But it was too late. The car took several turnings at full speed and Lumumba was soon on the highway.

Another car was waiting for us at the aerodrome. From there we began our journey to Stanleyville.

That evening we drove for more than two hundred kilometres along a muddy and bumpy road. We were stopped by the Kwilu River, where we had a small incident. The ferrymen flatly refused to take us across. We were surprised and asked them for the reason.

"It's the rule. We are not allowed to ferry Congolese after 10 p.m." Lumumba went to the ferrymen.

"Don't you know that there are new orders now, that the power in the land belongs to us? The Belgians no longer rule the Congo."

"That's true. But we've had no new instructions. That is why we are keeping the old rules."

One of the ferrymen raised his lantern and suddenly shouted in wild excitement: "It's Lumumba!"

There and then, on a piece of paper, Lumumba wrote instructions allowing Congolese to be ferried across the river' at any time. When we were on the far bank, he said sadly: "What a terrible heritage! They don't even realise that they can decide something themselves, that they are free. It will be difficult to work, but we will surmount everything and give the people knowledge. That is the main thing. It will be easier after that."

We drove all night and then, without resting, all day. Our plan to travel in secrecy failed. The people recognised Lumumba and warmly greeted him wherever our cars appeared. The news, relayed by "bamboo telegraph", that the Prime Minister was coming in person travelled from village to village faster than our cars. At Masi-Manimba, an administrative centre, the population showered Lumumba's car with flowers. Crowds of people barred our way. They brought us chicken, eggs and bananas to show that they were kindly disposed towards us. In many villages the people came out with weapons, thinking that Lumumba was mustering volunteers against the rebels. In Mangaya, at a rally that was held spontaneously, Lumumba said:

"Brothers, put away your weapons. But look after them, for you will need them. We shall have to fight for freedom. The colonialists don't want to give it to us peacefully, so we'll win it fighting them."

During a short halt, after we had crossed the Brabanta River, Lumumba talked to us round a fire. He spoke of the future unification of our forces, of a new army, of the need to rely on the people.

"You see, the people support the Government because our programme is clear: complete independence, the Congo for the Congolese. Fourteen million Congolese want work, a better future for their children. They want to be citizens with full political rights, they want a new life. The rebels are thinking of something totally different. At this moment they are calculating how much they'll get for their treachery. But the struggle hasn't ended. We shall gather new forces. I believe in my people."

I vividly remember this talk round the campfire. Lumumba's lucid thoughts cut deep into my memory. He said to me:

"You, Jacques, have contact with young people. That's from whom we get most of our support. Young people are eager

Page139

for a new life and this is a turning point for them. Either they'll get everything they want or they'll have to return to their back-breaking work in foreign-owned plantations, factories and mines. We must make them the masters of the country. Extensive organisational work is required. The young people have to be freed from tribal survivals and united round the idea of national unity, the rejuvenation of their country."

For me these words were the behest of a teacher. We never had another opportunity for a serious talk. We drove on and on, trying to get to Orientale Province as quickly as we could. There the people were waiting for Lumumba and he would be out of his pursuers' reach. At the Brabanta River we were joined by a group of Ministers and M.P.s. Now we were a big party and secrecy was out of the question. We knew that our pursuers were somewhere near.

At daybreak on November 30 we reached Port Francqui, where the administrator gave a luncheon in honour of the Prime Minister. People milled around the house, showing their friendliness. Suddenly a lorry full of troops drove up at full speed. They were rebels.

Although they were inclined to be bellicose, the presence of a large crowd made them hesitate to do anything. The sergeant in charge of the troops had a talk with Lumumba and demanded that he follow them. I do not know what was said because at the time I ran to a nearby U.N. post. The officer, an Englishman, listened to me coldly.

"We do not interfere in Congolese affairs," was his reply.

But the troops under him, all of whom were Africans, acted differently. Paying no attention to their officer, they quickly got their guns and ran to the administrator's house. That decided the issue. The rebels departed. The U.N. troops, riding in a lorry, accompanied us for about fifty kilometres and then waved us on.

We drove to the small town of Mweka. The commissioner met us on the road. Preparations for a rally were under way in the town. The people wanted to hear the Prime Minister. Lumumba hesitated. The danger had not passed, and the pursuit could be renewed. The Ministers insisted that he drive on. Out of the window of the car he looked thoughtfully at the square where several thousand people had already assembled.

"But what about them?" he said to us. "They're waiting to see me. I must say at least a few words to them."

The rally was held, and when it was ending we again saw our pursuers. This time the troops were driving in cars which the Belgians in Port Francqui had given them. We took a lightning decision. I jumped into Lumumba's black Chevrolet and sped along the highway to draw the attention of the troops. They gave chase, and in the meantime Lumumba and his companions went in a different direction, taking a roundabout route to the Sankuru River.

The Chevrolet was too fast for the troops. They halted somewhere along the highway, evidently giving up the chase, and turned back. At the entrance to Mweka they were awaited by a Belgian railway employee. He showed them where Lumumba went.

Lumumba and his companions were already far away. Towards seven in the evening they got to the tiny village of Lodi, where there was a ferry across the Sankuru. But the ferry boat was nowhere to be found. Lumumba decided to abandon the cars and cross the river in a canoe.

"We'll find other cars there, and if the worst comes to the worst we'll walk," he said to his companions.

There was only one canoe, and Lumumba and three companions crossed to the far bank first. Lumumba's wife and the rest of his party waited for the ferry boat. When the Prime Minister was already on the opposite bank, the pursuers suddenly appeared. The troops seized the entire party and shouted to Lumumba to return.

Without suspecting anything Lumumba got the ferrymen to cross the river and collect the people there. When the boat emerged from the darkness it was seized by troops, who crossed the river and surrounded Lumumba.

"Chief," the man in charge said, "we didn't want to cause you any harm. But they'll kill us if we return without you. You must understand it."

With a sad look at the soldiers Lumumba said:

"There's nothing to say. I know that to save yourselves you would murder Pauline and Roland. You can kill me. But remember—you'll never be forgiven. And you'll be sorry for the deed you're doing today."

Lumumba was sent to Mweka. I was there and saw a lorry with troops stop at the U.N. post on the town's outskirts at six in the morning. Lumumba, his hands tied behind his back, was standing in the lorry, and beside him were his wife, son, a Minister and several M.P.s. I ran to the British lieutenant.

"It's Lumumba, save him."

Lumumba himself said loudly and clearly from the lorry:

"Lieutenant, I am the Prime Minister. I request United Nations protection."

The lieutenant looked indifferently at him, crushed his cigarette and went into the house without replying. The rebel soldiers, who had watchfully waited for the results of Lumumba's appeal, seized Lumumba, dragged him out of the lorry and pushed him into a small red Opel that had come from Port Francqui.

I ran to the U.N. African troops. They raised the alarm and gave chase, but the red Opel was evidently too far away....

Whenever people now say that the U.N. could do nothing to prevent Lumumba's arrest, that its representatives did their utmost to stop his illegal detention, I remember that U.N. lieutenant, his haughty, indifferent face and the boot slowly crushing a smoking cigarette....

Source: *Patrice Lumumba: Fighter for Africa's Freedom*, Moscow, Progress Publishers, 1961, pp 104-110. **Written:** by Lev VOLODIN, Soviet journalist; **Transcribed:** by Thomas Schmidt.

A life given up for the people

Jean BULABEMBA

"There is no compromise between freedom and slavery," said Patrice Emery Lumumba, who sacrificed his life to bring real freedom to his people. Those who consider freedom as their exclusive prerogative murdered him in an effort to strangle Congolese nationalism.

"Africa will write her own history, and in both north and south it will be a history of glory and dignity," Lumumba wrote a few days before his death. The Congo already has its own history, but so far it is only a history of struggle, a history of a transitional period. The history of glory and dignity Lumumba spoke about will come.

Lumumba personifies the Congolese people. He chose the road of suffering, torture and, lastly, death rather than become a slave of the imperialists. He was firmly and deeply convinced that sooner or later his country would be completely independent. Like their leader, the Congolese people prefer to bear every form of suffering rather than see their freedom mutilated and trampled upon by those who for more than 80 years of colonial rule kept them in such poverty and bondage that they are themselves ashamed of it.

The Congolese people are carrying on their struggle for true independence.

LUMUMBA AND THE CONGOLESE PEOPLE

The movement for the Congo's liberation had its own features. At first, when real nationalists led by Lumumba demanded complete independence, some political leaders in connivance with colonialist circles called for the creation of a commonwealth with Belgium. Shorn of its trimmings, it meant the retention of colonial rule in the Congo pure and simple. One man realised earlier and better than any other political leader what had to be done to carry the national-liberation movement to victory. His name was Patrice Emery Lumumba and his prime concern was to make his people conscious of themselves as a nation.

He was the first Congolese leader to come into contact with the people, to discuss their country's problems with them and to take their will into consideration. In 1958, when he returned from Accra, he organised a rally in Leopoldville's Victory Square. More than 15,000 men, women, young people and old folk flocked to the square to listen to him. It was the first time in the Congo's history that the people responded to a call from a compatriot. Until then they had been taught to obey only the instructions of the white man.

The rally's success surpassed all expectations. I was there. With other Congolese political leaders standing beside him, Lumumba spoke of the Conference in Accra in a clear and simple manner. The people listened to him quietly and attentively.

Confident in himself and speaking off the cuff, he told the people of the difficulties lying on the road to independence. He repeatedly stressed the need for unity and national consciousness. "We are not unlike any other inhabitants of the world. The Congo is our country. We must be the masters in our homes. So let us this day begin the struggle for our rights. Let us unite and go forward to independence," he said.

The word "independence" struck a responsive chord in people's hearts. At that moment Lumumba established direct contact with his hearers. He had touched on their most cherished hopes. The people saw that he was the man to lead them to freedom. For his part Lumumba felt the response of his listeners.

He continued: "The colonialists seek to divide us in order to go on ruling us. Let us prove our maturity. Let us live like brothers. Independence is our birthright. We don't need anyone to present it to us because this country belongs to us. If the colonialists choose to ignore our lawful demands, we shall do everything to wrest our independence from them." The crowd responded with shouts of "Independence! Long live Lumumba! Independence!"

While the people voiced their heartfelt approval of Lumumba's statements, the few Belgians present in the square virtually writhed in fury. A Belgian official standing beside me turned purple with rage. In the meantime Lumumba went on speaking on the subject of national independence and the struggle to achieve it. Following Congolese custom, the speaker and his listeners began a dialogue. "Do you want to be the masters of your country?" Lumumba asked. "Yes," the people thundered in reply. "What is needed for that?" Lumumba continued. "Independence!" the people replied. This meeting, called for Congolese by Congolese, ended on a note of jubilation. Lumumba was the first man to awaken the people's national consciousness, which was to change the future of this old Belgian colony.

LUMUMBA AND THE CONGO'S POLITICAL LIFE

Naturally, the success of this Lumumba-organised rally required the continuation of political work among the people. Lumumba had no intention of tackling this task single-handed. He appealed to Congolese political leaders to unite in a single political bloc with independence as their common objective. He gave his political organisation the meaningful name of Congo National Movement (CNM), thereby underlining the aspiration for unity. Most of the political leaders responded favourably to Lumumba's appeal.

The colonialists attentively followed developments. Feeling the threat to their policy they immediately resorted to bribery. Huge sums of money passed into the hands of some political leaders on the understanding that they would break with Lumumba and oppose his efforts.

Drawing upon his own meagre resources, Lumumba toured the country and set up branches of the Congo National Movement which was gaining in popularity. The CNM's growing influence, due in large measure to Lumumba's efforts, furthered the development of the national-liberation movement in the Congo.

In Orientale Province support for the CNM was so overwhelming that branches were set up even in villages inhabited only by 20 persons or so. Lumumba personally toured the villages, speaking to the people. He knew several Congolese dialects and had no difficulty communicating with the people. He became the most popular figure in the country.

In the young states of Africa political activity requires exceptional endowments, particularly high spiritual qualities. The people loved Lumumba because they knew he shared their aspirations. Lumumba appreciated that political activity meant work with and among the people. He gave up a well-paid job and devoted himself entirely to politics. His travels about the country took him to the farthest corners. He appealed to the people and they responded to his appeals. He shared the unhappy lot of the Congolese nation and understood its sufferings, and the support he got from the people encouraged him to press for radical changes.

Throughout his career as a political leader Lumumba preached fraternal love between all Congolese. And he practised what he preached. When Kasavubu was arrested following the events of January 4, 1959, in Leopoldville, Lumumba took steps to obtain his release.

He looked for ways of forming an alliance with all Congolese leaders in order to begin a general offensive against the colonialists. In spite of the difficulties, he went to the people and said to them: "Let us continue the struggle. Let us be solidly behind our brothers who have been arrested by the colonialists in an effort to divide us."

LUMUMBA DIRECTS THE NATIONAL STRUGGLE FOR IMMEDIATE INDEPENDENCE

The political situation in the country grew tense after the arrests that followed the demonstration in Leopoldville on January 4, 1959. Developments in the Congo forced the Belgian Government to carry out a political and administrative reform.

This reform was announced in a declaration by the King and Government of Belgium on January 13, 1959. It mentioned independence.

The publication of this declaration sparked off a fresh upsurge of the struggle for national independence. The development of the national-liberation struggle depended on the positions adopted by the Congolese leaders. In this situation, the stand taken by Lumumba attracted nationwide attention and, in particular, the attention of Belgian political leaders.

Lumumba suggested convening a round-table conference of Belgian and Congolese leaders to work out the ways that would lead the Congo to immediate independence. The colonialists rejected his plan, refusing to talk with Congolese leaders whom they regarded as "unrepresentative".

The demand for a round-table conference received widespread support in Leopoldville and other major towns in the Congo. Lumumba's proposals were approved by all the nationalist leaders. At this decisive moment of the struggle for national independence Lumumba did his utmost to unite the efforts of all the political leaders. On his initiative, representatives of Congolese political parties gathered together several times to work out a common policy. Lumumba, of course, played an important role in these quests for a joint line and greatly influenced the decisions that were taken.

When the Belgian authorities flatly refused to meet the Congolese leaders, whom they continued to regard as "unrepresentative", Lumumba appealed to the people to go out into the streets and peaceably demonstrate their aspiration for freedom.

In 1959 he organised two congresses. CNM leaders gathered at the first congress, and at the second all the nationalist parties reached agreement on a joint plan of action.

The CNM congress was held at a time when it was obvious that the colonialists would try to start disorders. While the congress was in session in the large hall of the Mangobo Commune in Stanleyville, Belgian-officered soldiers and gendarmes patrolled the street outside. The presence of the soldiers in no way cooled passions, but Lumumba succeeded in avoiding any worsening of the situation. He constantly called upon the population to remain calm and warned them against provocateurs. The congress adopted resolutions demanding independence without delay, the Africanisation of personnel and an immediate meeting between Congolese and Belgian leaders.

Lumumba hardly slept at all during the days the congress was in session. After the sittings he could be seen in the secretariat offices, typing and helping out in other ways. He received delegations, discussed various problems with congress delegates and other visitors, wrote statements for the press and held press conferences.

At this time there was tension between the civilian population and troops commanded by Belgian officers. This tension reached white heat when the congress of the nationalist parties opened. Lumumba went to Leroy, the governor of Orientale Province, and warned him that the behaviour of the army, which was in a mood to fire upon the crowds, was fraught with dangerous consequences.

On Lumumba's suggestion the congress sent a telegram to the Belgian Government demanding that the colonial authorities arrange a meeting between Congolese and Belgian leaders without delay. The Belgian Government replied that it had no intention whatever of discussing the Congo's future with Congolese leaders. The reply came in the evening. The congress had hoped it would be more or less favourable. After reading the telegram, Lumumba said: "I propose we break with Belgium," and the delegates unanimously shouted their approval.

The Belgian officers observing the congress through the windows broke into the premises and threw tear-gas bombs. Lumumba courageously went to the Belgians and told them to leave the hall. It was the first time in the history of the Belgian colony that white officers were compelled to obey an African.

Lumumba's courageous behaviour won the warm approval of the crowds outside. More and more people filled the street. In the face of the provocative actions of the troops, the people of Stanleyville armed themselves with spears, bows and arrows, knives and other weapons. The situation was becoming tense. The Belgian officers completely lost control over themselves and began to fire at the crowd after the Congolese soldiers refused to fire at their brothers. When the first Congolese was struck down by the officers' bullets, Lumumba went to the dead man, lifted him in his arms and wept. The sight of Lumumba weeping with bullets whistling in the air round him made the people reply to the fire of the Belgian officers. Some of the officers fell to the ground, their hearts pierced by arrows. Lumumba wished to stop further bloodshed, and in this confusion he called upon the people to remain calm. They obeyed him and dispersed, leaving the street to the troops.

Disturbances broke out again that night. Lumumba was somewhere at the other end of the city, and when he arrived at the trouble spot it was already too late. Dead troops and civilians, black and white, lay on the road. The authorities ordered ruthless repressions. A warrant for Lumumba's arrest was issued on the next day. The news of Lumumba's arrest spread like wildfire in Leopoldville, capital of the Congo. The colonialists desperately looked for support among the Congolese leaders, but they could find very little of it. The rallies organised by the CNM drew huge crowds. Resolutions supporting Lumumba were sent to Brussels. Delegations of the different strata of the population went to the Belgian authorities in the Congo and demanded Lumumba's immediate release.

Daily the political situation worsened. The elections to local organs of power, set for the end of 1959, drew near. The nationalist parties decided to boycott these elections. Though in prison, Lumumba continued to direct the activities of his supporters, and his letters reached their destinations despite the close surveillance. Naturally, he was assisted by

Congolese troops. It is interesting to note that in spite of the strict measures that were taken by the colonial authorities, almost all of these troops were members of the CNM and had party membership cards.

LUMUMBA AND THE BRUSSELS ROUND-TABLE CONFERENCE

In January 1960, the Belgian Government convened a round-table conference in Brussels. It was attended by Congolese leaders and Belgian representatives. At the time the conference opened Lumumba was transferred from Stanleyville to a prison in Jadotville that was notorious as a torture chamber. He was barefoot, handcuffed and bore the marks of beatings. He had been manhandled on the way.

The Brussels conference opened without Lumumba, but his representatives were there. The proceedings dragged on for several days without any agreement being reached. The Congolese leaders made it plain to the Belgian authorities that the conference would break down unless the repressions against Congolese were stopped and Lumumba was permitted to attend the conference. This condition was complied with.

In Brussels Lumumba was met by the majority of the Congolese leaders and journalists. He showed them his wounds. In a statement to the press he appealed to the Belgians and Congolese to reach agreement on the early achievement of independence by the Congo.

His presence at the round-table conference cleared the atmosphere. He played a particularly noteworthy role in naming the day for the proclamation of independence. At the conference he publicly exposed the manoeuvres of some Belgian financial groups, who were seeking to split the Congolese and thereby divide the Congo. He even walked out of the conference, and only returned when Tshombe's lawyer, a Belgian named Humblet, was excluded from its sittings. He realised that the objective was to legalise Katanga's secession and called attention to the danger. The other Congolese leaders supported him and condemned the activities of Tshombe, who in view of the general discontent was compelled to give assurances that he had never advocated Katanga's secession. But subsequent events showed that this was a lie.

An Executive Council, which included Congolese members, was set up during the round-table conference on Lumumba's suggestion. This Council was attached to the Governor-General of the Congo and, in principle, its job was to help prepare the proclamation of independence and the parliamentary elections.

Upon their return to the Congo the national leaders were given a jubilant reception by the people. The Congolese were proud that their leaders had been successful. An election campaign began. Lumumba won the election in April 1960. This was frowned upon by the colonialists, who did their utmost to keep Lumumba away from power. But they came up against the people's determination, against Congolese reality. In spite of all their intrigues, Lumumba became the Prime Minister of the Republic of the Congo. His deputy was Antoine Gizenga, who later carried on his work.

LUMUMBA AND THE CONGO'S INDEPENDENCE

The colonialists' plots aimed at giving the country only formal independence were exposed by Lumumba long before June 30, 1960, the day the independence of the Republic of the Congo was proclaimed. He went to the people, explaining the political situation to them and uniting them. Rallies were held all over the country. Lumumba secured a basic agreement among the nationalist parties with regard to unity of action. These parties subsequently formed the Lumumba or nationalist bloc.

On June 30, 1960, when the people of the Congo were celebrating their independence, the Belgians were already dreaming of regaining control over the country. But in spite of all their intrigues against Lumumba, he remained in power right up to the grimmest period of his political career.

Six days after independence was proclaimed, the. people of the Congo ran into an emergency precipitated by the colonialists. Everybody knows what that emergency was. In those days and right up to the last minute of his life, Lumumba showed he was a great leader guiding the destinies of his people whom he had always served devotedly.

Lumumba's life was a continuous struggle for the Congo's interests. With the support of the people he became the Head of Government and the leader of the national-liberation movement in the country. Today, when he is dead, his people remember him, his cause and his life.

We are confident that the righteous cause for which many of the Congo's sons have given their lives will ultimately triumph.

*Source: **Patrice Lumumba: Fighter for Africa's Freedom**,*
*Moscow, Progress Publishers, 1961, pp 80-90. **Written:** by Jean*
BULABEMBA, Congolese journalist;
***Transcribed:** by Thomas Schmidt.*

Such was Lumumba

Yuri ZHUKOV

I am writing these lines at night. The teletype is ticking away, hurrying to overtake time. Coils of yellowish tape filled with tiny letters steadily pile up as a violent storm of news rages in the ether: the whole world is turbulently protesting against the murder of Lumumba. And out of this tempest comes a brief cynical dispatch from Elisabethville via New York, stating that Lumumba's body had been burnt. One of Mobutu's airmen, a certain Jack Dixon, who transported the captive Lumumba to Elisabethville, told correspondents: "They tore the hair from his head and tried to force him to eat it...."

They tore the hair from his head and tried to force him to eat it. I do not know who this airman with the Anglo-Saxon name is, but his cold-blooded and inhumanly unemotional description of the tortures to which the man he was taking to the executioner was subjected sounds like something out of S.S. records.

As I gazed at this unevenly torn piece of teletype, somewhere in the distance I saw the proud and energetic face of a great man who remained unconquerable no matter how he was tortured, and who, even after his death, struck such fear in the hearts of his executioners that they hastily burnt his body and scattered the ashes. As I looked back I felt I could not resist the temptation to describe my meetings with this fascinating man during the days when Hammarskjöld's sleek officials were bowing to him with servile smiles, when the misfit reporter Mobutu, who by a turn of destiny became Chief-of-Staff, vowed fidelity, and the Judas Bomboko, who was hatching a conspiracy, was following him like a shadow.

We arrived in Leopoldville in the latter half of August 1960 to discuss cultural relations with the Minister of Education of the Congo: the young republic was asking for doctors, for aid to organise the training of specialists in the Congo herself and abroad, and technical assistance to repair a radio station, whose transmitter had been partially put out of commission by the colonialists when they left Leopoldville.

After a long non-stop flight, our aircraft landed on the splendid concrete-paved runway of a modern aerodrome. There was a deathly stillness when the screaming of the motors died down. It seemed as though we had landed on an uninhabited island. With the exception of several big-bellied U.S. military transport planes used to airlift U.N. troops to the Congo, the aerodrome was deserted. We pushed open the door of our aircraft and found that we had to solve the problem of how to climb down to the ground. While we debated this problem we saw a gangway moving slowly in our direction. It was being pushed by several men, black and white. They made friendly gestures.

Soon we found that they were Pierre Mulele, Minister of Education, a thin young man with a small curly beard, and officials from the Soviet Embassy who had come to meet us. The U.N. officials in charge of the aerodrome had by this time dismissed the entire personnel of the aerodrome and were doing nothing to return things to normal. We were given a very warm welcome and were soon sitting in the Minister's close office and talking of everyday and yet very important matters....

Driving past the Parliament building, we saw the flags of many African countries waving over the entrance. A conference of leading public figures of the Congo, Ghana, Guinea, the Cameroons, Togo, Ethiopia, Liberia, the Sudan, Morocco, the United Arab Republic and Angola had just been opened in the Congolese capital by the Prime Minister Patrice Lumumba. On the next day we read his courageous and moving speech in the newspaper *Congo*, which has the words "The first Congolese daily newspaper owned by Africans" splashed across the top of the front page.

"For my government, for all of us Congolese," he said to the delegates, "your presence here at this moment is living proof of African reality, the reality that our enemies have always disallowed. But you know that this reality is stubborn and that Africa is hale and hearty. It refuses to die.... We all know and the whole world knows that Algeria is not French, that Angola is not Portuguese, that Kenya is not British, that Ruanda-Urundi is not Belgian.... We know what the West is aiming at. Yesterday they split us up on the level of tribes and clans. Today, when Africa is steadfastly liberating itself, they want to divide us on the level of states. In Africa they seek to set up opposing blocs, satellite states and then, on that basis, to start a 'cold war', to widen the split and to perpetuate their trusteeship. But I know that Africa wants to be united and that it will not give way to these machinations...."

In the meantime Leopoldville was taking on the appearance of a besieged city. Military trucks and jeeps filled with helmeted soldiers armed with automatic rifles and submachine-guns sped across the deserted streets of the city. The colour of the helmets showed who these troops were: red-stripped white helmets were worn by the military police, dark-green helmets by the armed forces of the Congolese Republic and blue helmets by the U.N. force. There was unrest at the big Leopold military camp, which for some time now was attracting the special attention of correspondents.

There was hardly any discipline in the camp: the men were openly grumbling that they were not getting their pay and that the food was bad. Their wives, who lived with them, complained that they had nothing to feed their children with. Mobutu, the Chief-of-Staff, whose duty it was to restore order and supply the army with all elementary necessaries, was playing a double-game: he vowed loyalty to the government, promising an early offensive against Katanga, where the traitor Tshombe had entrenched himself, and at the same time was doing all in his power to turn the soldiers against the Prime Minister....

In the evening the Prime Minister gave a dinner for the delegates to the All-African Conference. The entire diplomatic corps and foreign visitors to Leopoldville were invited. A military band played in a shady flood-lit garden on the bank of the mighty African river. The envoys of the different African countries, dressed in their colourful costumes, began to arrive. The ambassadors of the Western countries were present, dressed in tuxedoes and frock-coats. Some of them tried to make a show of courtesy but did not always succeed. The guests were met by the Prime Minister, a lanky man of about thirty-five. His energetic, animated face instantly impresses itself on one's memory—the piercing, glowing brown eyes that reflect profound assurance and spiritual dignity seem to look into your very soul.

This man appeared on the political scene very recently, only three years ago. But these were years of intense activity, years when he and his friends acquired tremendous experience.

Upon being told that we were from Moscow, Lumumba warmly greeted us and invited us to come to see him on the next day. At the reception we met some of Lumumba's friends: Deputy Prime Minister Gizenga, a short, cool and sober-minded man; the young and cheerful Minister for Youth Affairs and Sports Mpolo; and the somberish Minister of Information Anicet Kashamura, who said that the Belgian specialists still working in his Ministry were giving him a pain in the neck.

I sat at the same table with a Guinean delegate in long snow-white robes and a Moslem fez. In front of us sat the ambassador of a Western country with an absent-minded smile on his face and the Minister of Foreign Affairs Bom-boko, dressed in a tuxedo. He was playing the role of a genial host who deeply regretted that due to circumstances beyond his control his guests were not really enjoying themselves.

"Of course," he was saying to his neighbour with much agitation, "as a civilised person I am revolted at the policy of unjustified arrests. But what can I do? You must understand my position...."

"You're right in principle," my neighbour suddenly responded. "But not one of the Western correspondents, who write so much about unjustified arrests, has yet been able to give a single concrete example. Don't you think, Your Excellency, that a few arrests would be justified here in Leopoldville? Our friend Patrice Lumumba is much too generous."

Bomboko frowned and grew silent, concentrating on the food before him. Meanwhile, the Prime Minister rose and took the floor. He spoke with passion, like the born orator he was. He said that the movement for freedom and unity that was now sweeping across Africa was irreversible. An end would be put to the colonial system once and for all. He called upon the representatives of the Western Powers to show a sober understanding of reality and to co-operate with the Republic of the Congo as with an equal partner.

"We stretch out our hand to everybody who desires such co-operation," he said, "to the Americans and to the Russians, to the French and the British, and even to the Belgians, if they are prepared to stop their intervention."

The Western guests smiled courteously, but from the expressions on their faces it was obvious that what the Prime Minister said was not to their liking. My neighbour leaned over to me and whispered in my ear:

"You can't expect anything good from them. Mark my words, Lumumba is standing on ceremony with their agents to no purpose. He shouldn't have forgiven Bomboko and some other people after their conspiracy was exposed."

The band struck up again. Waiters noiselessly served ice-cream on dishes with ice-cubes covered with the blue flames of burning rum. On the surface everything seemed to be quiet and peaceful. Bomboko smiled at the guests, the ambassadors were engaged in polished chatter. The Commander of the Armed Forces Victor Lundula, who fought against the Nazis in the Second World War, alone had no ear for all this conviviality. Dressed in a coarse grey cloth suit, he kept rising from his table and returning, and messengers kept running up to him. As we learnt later, troops were moved to the borders of Katanga Province while the reception was in progress. A military clash was becoming imminent in that province. At the time we knew nothing of this nor of the fact that the Chief-of-Staff Mobutu, that uncommonly thin man in large spectacles who was meekly reporting something to Lundula, was preparing the operation in such a way as to send all troops loyal to Lumumba to the south and to leave in Leopoldville only those men, who, led by Belgian officers carrying on underground, would not stop at overthrowing the legal government….

In the morning we went to the Prime Minister's residence, a small house on the bank of the Congo River, in which tiny islands of vegetation were floating by. Gay children's voices could be heard behind the thickly overgrown fence. Curly-headed youngsters were sliding down the banister of the porch. They were the Prime Minister's children; with a curiosity that was mingled with pride they gazed at the helmeted sentries armed with submachine-guns and standing rigidly as though they were statues: the children could not yet get used to seeing their father guarded by such important personages.

The little drawing-room was filled with scores of people seeking an audience with the

Prime Minister. You could feel they had been waiting for a long time. In vain did the tired secretary try to persuade them to take their affairs to the pertinent ministries. They insisted on seeing Lumumba: the merchant who wanted a license for his business, the official applying for a transfer to another town and the teacher asking for a rise in his salary. The state apparatus of the young republic had not yet been knit together properly—there was still a lack of experience, and a multitude of cares distracted the Prime Minister from affairs of state.

We were taken to Lumumba through a back entrance, where, incidentally, there was also a crowd of people trying to slip through to the Prime Minister. When we entered his office, Lumumba dismissed the large group of officials crowding round his desk, which was piled high with papers and books, and sat down beside us on an old divan. Our conversation was interrupted time and again by telephone calls. People rang him up on all matters and every minute there was something he had to look into and settle.

While Lumumba spoke over the telephone we looked round his small and simply furnished study. An automatic rifle lay within easy reach on a shelf. There was a portable radio transmitter. After two plots to murder him had been uncovered the Prime Minister has been compelled to take certain precautions.

There was an infinitely weary look on his face, but his eyes continued to burn with indomitable energy. He had not slept at all in the past twenty-four hours and yet he was planning to fly to Stanleyville in the evening to be on hand to meet the Soviet aircraft bringing foodstuffs that the Government of the Soviet Union was sending as a gift to the people of the Congo. Two members of the government, Lumumba told us, were going to the port of Matadi to receive the Soviet Lorries that were coming by ship.

> "We greatly appreciate this aid," the Prime Minister said with feeling, "as a testimony of the friendship that your people have for us. I would like you to tell Soviet people that what they have done for us during these difficult days will never be forgotten."

Lumumba eagerly questioned us about the results of our talks with the Minister of Education. He wanted the republic to have cultural relations with all countries, the Soviet Union included. He spoke with pain and anger of the backwardness into which the colonialists had forced his people. The colonialists had made fabulous fortunes by shamelessly exploiting the country's colossal deposits of uranium, gold, diamonds, copper and coal. And what had they given in return?

During the period of their rule the population had decreased by almost fifty per cent. Starvation and disease were rife. The Congolese people now had to begin building up their country from the beginning and required immense aid. But where was that aid to come from? The government of the republic had expected much from the U.N., when it had open-heartedly asked it to send an international force to drive the colonialists out of the country and help restore order. But it looked as if by inviting this force the Congolese had got themselves out of the frying-pan only to fall into the fire. Hammarskjöld was behaving in much the same way as King Baudouin had....

The Prime Minister smiled bitterly. His long nervous fingers twitched: he was deeply agitated by what was happening. The U.N. force was at one with the colonialists. No sooner would the government uncover one plot than another would be hatched. Out of a feeling of tact Lumumba avoided mentioning the principal plotter, Kasavubu, the President of the Republic. It was no secret that this man, a product of the Belgian Catholic mission schools, was the chief stooge of the colonialists and that instigated by them he was planning the overthrow of the government....

The Prime Minister spoke of the problems that he was now working on to start the country's development: the creation of a network of hospitals, the preparations for the coming school year, the problem of where and how many young people to send to turn them into the highly trained specialists so acutely needed by the country, the problem of strengthening the state apparatus....

He described the cordial reception that the All-African Conference gave to the message sent to it by Soviet Prime Minister Khrushchev.

"That's who our real and sincere friend is," Lumumba said. "I have never met him personally, but I hope we shall meet some day. Please tell Mr. Khrushchev that our people thank him with all their hearts for his concern and support. We are confident that friendly relations based on mutual respect of each other's sovereignty will develop between our countries. The imperialists are doing their utmost to disrupt the Security Council's decision on the withdrawal of Belgian troops from the Congo. We Africans are, perhaps, still naive, but we sincerely believed in the U.N. Charter and hoped that it would be observed by the nations that had signed it. That was why we approached that organisation for help. But look what came of it?"

Again a bitter smile came to his lips and he spread out his arms. An angry spark suddenly lit up his eyes.

> "Never mind. Perhaps this will cost us dearly, very dearly, but the lesson will be learned by Africa. The peoples of Africa will realise who are our friends and who our enemies and how to distinguish between them....
>
> "We are not enemies of any country," Lumumba continued, "and we are prepared to co-operate with all countries. I made myself sufficiently clear on this point yesterday. But we are against oppression and exploitation. We did not free ourselves from bondage to the Belgians simply in order to put another yoke round our necks. No matter how events shape out, even if they will be unfavourable for us, it will be useful for Africa, which is now watching us and closely following what is happening here—it will be a university of struggle for it...."

He was about to add something, but the door opened with a bang and a group of military men strode into the room. They spoke excitedly in their own language.

The Prime Minister rose and, turning to me, said quietly in French:

> "You must excuse me but something important has just happened. A group of Belgian officers in civilian dress have landed on the aerodrome. The U.N. has taken over control of the aerodrome on the pretext that that is a necessary step to avert civil war. We were told that it was a 'neutralising' operation. Now you see what that word means. We are now going to catch those Belgian scoundrels...."

He repeated his request that we convey his heartfelt greetings and gratitude to the head of the Soviet Government, said good-bye, quickly walked out into the street, sat in a jeep filled with soldiers and drove off to the aerodrome.

I never had another opportunity of speaking to him, but I shall always remember this fearless and strong man, his expressive face with the small jet-black goatee, his big and deeply human sparkling eyes, his quick gestures, his light and fast gait, and his unique manner of speaking with clipped phrases and accentuated intonations that reflected his deep conviction of the righteousness of every word he spoke.

He was a remarkable man in every respect and had his life not been cut short at the very beginning of his political career by those who feared him, he would, undoubtedly, have become one of the most outstanding personalities of our epoch. A man of talent and will, he could find his way out of the most difficult situations. Recall how on three occasions in succession, when his enemies were already preparing to celebrate their victory, he sharply changed the most impossible situations and invariably proved to be the master.

Following up his coup, Mobutu sent his picked cutthroats to arrest Lumumba. The Prime Minister opened their eyes for them and they went away feeling that the man who should have been seized was the one who had signed the warrant for the arrest of the Prime Minister.

Mobutu imprisoned Lumumba at the Leopold military camp. There Lumumba spoke to the soldiers. They cheered him and he left the camp in triumph.

Mobutu again seized him and held him in captivity in another camp, in Thysville. There, too, Lumumba showed his jailers that his was the just cause and they again released him.

Mobutu hurried to turn his indomitable captive over to the hangman Tshombe in Katanga Province, and there he was murdered.

But even in death Lumumba cows his executioners. As I write these lines crowds of angry people are gathering outside Belgian embassies throughout the world and protesting against the crime perpetrated in far-away Katanga. In Cairo infuriated demonstrators broke into the Belgian Embassy, where they tore down the portraits of King Baudouin and put up portraits of Lumumba in their stead: his eyes looked wrathfully through the glasses, reducing to ashes those who were seeking to restore the colonial yoke in Africa.

Such was Lumumba. Even after death he remained in the ranks of his people, who are continuing their struggle for freedom.

Source: Patrice Lumumba, The Truth about a Monstrous Crime of the Colonialists, Moscow, Foreign Languages Publishing House, 1961, pp. 89-99.
Written: by Yuri ZHUKOV;
Transcribed: by Thomas Schmidt.

The goal Patrice sought to achieve

N. KHOKHLOV

The whole of mankind now sees the Belgian colonialists as vicious plunderers. The myth that the former Belgian Congo was a model colony has collapsed. In the African continent Brussels had seized a whole country, pillaging it for nearly 80 years. During this long period Belgian writers produced a huge number of books on this vast tropical colony. Fat tomes and slim brochures importunately preached the single idea that the modern Congo had been created by the monarchs in Brussels. Like the Lord in Heaven who is supposed to have created everything terrestrial, the Belgian kings "created" an entire country. "Without kings, without Belgium there would have been no Congo!" the imperialist pen-pushers cried from the roof-tops. That, in essence, was how the Congolese nation was robbed spiritually. That was the substance of colonial propaganda. What official Brussels called its "civilising mission" was nothing but brigandage and the forbidding reality of the capitalist world.

The Congo is one of the oldest countries in Africa. Its name is derived from the Congo, which is one of the greatest rivers of the world. The country has a territory of 905 square miles, which is 77 times bigger than the territory of Belgium. It turns out that a small European colonial vulture conquered and exploited a territory that is almost 80 times the size of the kingdom of Belgium.

A census has never been taken of the population of the Congo. The colonialists estimated the number of inhabitants "by eye". It is believed that in the Congo today there are at least 14 million inhabitants. Historians assert that the population of the Congo decreased by half in the past century, i.e., during the period of Belgian domination. In the recent past the Congo was one of the main sources of slaves for the West. Historical researches point to the astounding fact that European traders in "live merchandise" shipped over 13 million slaves from the Congo. More than five million unfortunate inhabitants of Equatorial Africa perished in the voyages across the Atlantic.

In the African languages the Congo means "Great Water". The earliest mention of this far-away and fabulously rich country is to be found in the notes of the Carthaginian Hanno and the Arab navigator Pateneit. The numerous peoples of the Congo had their own highly developed culture, which was almost completely effaced by the strangers from Europe, who took from the Congo everything they could: people, rare species of trees, gold and pearls, ivory and the skins of rare animals. Henry Morton Stanley, who is also referred to as one of the "creators" of the Congo, wrote:

"Every tusk, piece and scrap in the possession of an Arab trader has been steeped and dyed in blood. Every pound weight has cost the life of a man, woman or child, for every five pounds a hut has been burnt, for every two tusks a whole village has been destroyed, every twenty tusks have been obtained at the price of a district with all its people, villages and plantations."

In the period between 1857 and 1876 alone, nearly 800 Tons of ivory was shipped out of Africa annually. In other words, the colonialist barbarians destroyed not less than 51,000 elephants a year.

No one can say how much precious metal was taken out of the Congo or give the quantity of diamonds that was wrung out of the diamond-fields scattered along the Kasai and Lulua rivers. It would be an impossible task to state the number of ships that sailed away loaded with ebony and jacaranda, with baobab and sequoia, with bamboo, or with crocodile skins. The Baluba people have no other name for a Belgian than *pene toto*, which means "money-grabbing". For a piece of copper wire or for a handful of glass beads that were used as ornaments by tribal chiefs, the Belgian colonialist received in exchange bags of gold dust and bottles filled with diamonds. He killed hippopotamuses and crocodiles, giraffes and deer, leopards and the rare okapis.

For a song he acquired the priceless masks of the Bashi, Lulua and Baluba tribes and bought up the works by artists of the *poto-poto* school, which is famous throughout Africa. The Brussels merchants began to bring from the Congo even giant canoes hollowed out of the ancient trees growing on the banks of the great African river. Jungles were cut down and the dense, luxuriant forests were laid waste. The once flourishing flora and fauna began to grow sickly. The Congo became a "dying land".

The bronze statues of Belgian kings, sticking into the air in Leopoldville, Luluabourg, Bukavu, Stanleyville, Elisabethville, Matadi, Boma and many other Congolese towns are unique landmarks of pillage and colonial piracy. Leopold II issued an edict decreeing the chopping-off of the hands of Congolese who did not bring the fixed amount of rubber, coffee or ivory. To this day one can meet in the Congo old men with amputated left hands as sinister reminders of the Belgian monarch. Who was left-handed lost his right hand.

Since those days Belgian "civilisation" has changed to some extent, taking on a more "modern" appearance. The Congolese no longer had their hands mutilated: they were savagely flogged instead. There were purely mercantile considerations behind this fiendish "humanity":

it was unprofitable to chop off a man's hands as that deprived him of his capacity for work. The colonialists turned to the whip and lash.

The Congo is a grim reproach to and a stern accusation of the colonial system of oppression. Occupying a twelfth part of the territory of Africa, the Congo lived in darkness and her people were doomed to extinction. A handful of Belgian magnates wallowed in wealth while the population of the tropics knew nothing but hardship and privation. The Belgian Union Minière controls billions of francs, but the Congolese does not have two francs with which to buy a box of matches. After a few years in the Congo, the Belgian official builds luxurious villas, buys the latest American cars and can command a comfortable life for the rest of his days. A Congolese has to work for a year to earn the price of an aircraft ticket from Leopoldville to Elisabethville. An American car costs from 220,000 to 250,000 francs, a sum that a Congolese can never earn even in 50 or 60 years.

Many of the Belgians in the Congo have private helicopters, sea-going vessels and launches, to say nothing of cars. The Congolese has what his grandfather and great-grandfather had before him: a wretched hut made of bamboo and palm leaves, a ragged singlet and a loin-cloth. The Belgian imports wild goat meat into the Congo from the Portuguese colony of

Angola, drinks the choicest of French wines and treats himself to oysters brought in refrigerators from Antwerp. The food the Congolese eats consists of manioc, which, ground into flour, was eaten by the local inhabitants a hundred, two hundred and a thousand years ago.

The colonialists enmeshed the glorious Congolese people in chains of spiritual slavery. When I went to the Congo I wanted to meet Congolese writers, scientists, doctors and teachers. But there were none to meet. This former Belgian colony with its population of 14 million people does not have a single doctor, scientist or teacher of its own. What an unspeakable disgrace this is to civilised and cultured Belgium! In the Congo not a single newspaper is published in the local language: all publications belong to the Belgian Catholics.

The French language has trampled and supplanted the Lingala, Ki-Kongo, Chikoba and Kiswahili languages that are spoken by millions of people. Brussels eradicated the whole of Congolese culture, flinging a many-million-strong people into the abyss of medieval darkness. This was the modern barbarism that Patrice Lumumba, ardent patriot and great son of his people, struggled against. The nation spoke through his lips, declaring relentless war on colonialism. Lumumba sacrificed his life for a united, sovereign Congo. His ideals live in the hearts of Congolese patriots, who are determined to consummate these bright ideals in the name of which a hero of our day has died.

* * *

The horrible news that Patrice Emery Lumumba was murdered in cold blood in the Katanga lair was for all of us like a blow by a home-made Congolese battle-axe. The destiny of this heroic man, a devoted patriot and an ardent fighter against the accursed colonial regime, is inseparable from the destiny of his homeland. Patrice, as he is lovingly and simply called by the Congolese people, was always in the front ranks of the patriots who courageously and proudly bid defiance to the imperialist vultures. The tragedy of Lumumba as a politician, man and fighter reflects the bottomless grief of the 14-million-strong Congolese people. The Congo and Lumumba, Lumumba and the Congo are interlaced and each of them stirs us and evokes vehement hatred for the organisers of this orgy of blood.

Who was Patrice Lumumba? What were the ideals to which he was dedicated heart and soul?

Lumumba was born on July 2, 1925, in Sankuru Region, Kasai Province. He belonged to the Mutetela ethnical group. After finishing secondary school he went to work, finding employment in various colonial firms and offices. He was a post-office employee and worked in a factory run by a Belgian. At the same time he plunged into literary and journalistic activity, writing poems and publishing articles about the terrible plight of the Congolese. In Stanleyville he founded the newspaper *Uhuru (Freedom)*, which today is one of the most popular in the Congo Republic. Lumumba was the director of the weekly *Indepéndance*. In October 1959, he published a declaration on the establishment of the Congo National Movement Party. This was the organizational culmination of the extensive work that was done by Lumumba and his associates to mobilise and unite into a single party all the progressive forces standing shoulder to shoulder in the liberation movement. The Party advanced the slogan of "Independence Now!"

The Belgian colonialists flung Lumumba into jail twice. But long before independence was proclaimed Lumumba's popularity and influence among his people was such that it could not be ignored by the official Brussels. The Belgian King had a long conversation with Lumumba during one of his visits to the Congo. Lumumba was promised a high position and an untroubled life in a new pro-Belgian and, essentially, colonial government of the Congo. Lumumba remained true to his political convictions and with unflagging energy went on defending the rights of the enslaved Congolese people.

It is characteristic that in the elections in Orientale Province Lumumba's Party received 90 per cent of the votes. This took place at a time when the leader of the Party was in jail.

The so-called round-table conference, held in the Belgian capita) early in 1960, was planned by official Brussels as a rehearsal to determine the role Congolese leaders would play in the future "independent" government at Leopoldville. The colonial officials had already selected "suitable" candidates: Jean Bolikango, for example, could be president, and Joseph Kasavubu prime minister.

The conference organisers endeavoured to avoid even the mention of Lumumba's name. But the plan hatched in Brussels was upset as soon as the conference began. Lumumba's supporters demanded that the head of the Congo National Movement Party be admitted to the conference.

"If Lumumba is not invited we shall leave Brussels," Congolese patriots declared.

Lumumba was in jail at the time. The Belgians had no alternative but to release him immediately and bring him to Brussels by aircraft. It is said that when Lumumba entered the conference room his arms still bore the bloody marks of shackles: they had been taken off only a few hours before.

In Leopoldville I, like all the other Soviet correspondents, saw Lumumba many times, went to his residence and attended his press conferences. I would say that simplicity and fidelity to principles are the qualities that distinguish Patrice Lumumba most of all. He began one of his press conferences with the words:

> "I have invited you, gentlemen, to talk with you, to seek your advice and to exchange opinions. I hope that you will be objective in reporting the events in my country and keep world opinion informed of the truth."

That was Lumumba's way—warm and stimulating.

There was no correspondent in Leopoldville who did not have the greatest of respect for Lumumba. Everything about this outstanding personality was attractive: his ardent calls against colonialism, his passion as a political leader and his ability to engage an adversary in open and honest battle. Here is what the British *Foreign Report* wrote about this remarkable leader of the Congo:

"Hard-working, physically courageous and a charmer, his strength is that he is the only genuinely nationalist, anti-tribal and anti-regional Congolese leader.... Mr. Lumumba seems to be the only Congolese politician with the necessary ambition and qualities to hold the Congo together as a unitary state."

Lumumba showed that he was a convinced and consistent opponent of tribalism, of tribal wars. A native of Kasai, which is inhabited by dozens of ethnical groups, tribes and nationalities, Lumumba knew what the tribal wars cost the Congolese people and time and again urged that an end be put to hostility between tribes once and for all. The membership of Lumumba's Party is a practical embodiment of his ideas, for it embraces almost all the nationalities of the Congo and there are branches of his Party in every province.

Patrice Lumumba worked in an exceedingly difficult situation. The treasury was empty. There was no national army. The state apparatus was weak. The government had no means of transportation. There had been several cases of Belgian aircraft taking off with Lumumba on board only to return to the airport after circling over it. The colonialists resorted to base means to deprive the Prime Minister of all opportunity of touring the republic and speaking to the people.

"Westerners and U.N. representatives are the only people I meet," Lumumba said in such cases. "I have to speak French, when all the time I yearn to discuss things in my native Lingala, to meet with the peasants."

Yes, with his people he spoke in Lingala. Those were stirring scenes! When he arrived in Stanleyville, tens of thousands of townsfolk and villagers came to meet him. The Elaeis palms seemed to shake with the mighty shouts of:

"Congo! Lumumba! *Uhuru!*"

In Stanleyville I saw that if you wanted to make a Congolese smile and well disposed towards you had to greet him with just the one word *Lumumba*.

Lumumba showed a very eager interest in the Soviet Union. He was always glad to meet and talk with Soviet people. While in Stanleyville, he found the time to talk with Vasily Shishkin, head of a team of Soviet doctors who worked in the province. He asked how the Soviet doctors were getting used to the tropical climate, what accommodations they had, how they were supplied with food, and so on.

"You come straight to me if you have difficulties," he said to Shishkin.

Lumumba was the one who said that the Soviet Union was the only Great Power whose position was in accord with the will and views of the Congolese people. This evaluation of the Soviet Union's policy of disinterestedly supporting the fighting people of the Congo served as grounds for accusing Lumumba of favouring communism. He was asked about this during receptions in Leopoldville and during his trips abroad. His reply was:

> "We are neither Communists, Catholics nor socialists. We are African nationalists. We reserve the right to choose our friends in accordance with the principle of positive neutrality."

Lumumba had the uncanny gift of instantaneously exposing the plots of the enemies of a united Congo, The local and overseas colonialists alike feared his speeches. Hammarskjöld preferred not to meet him: the U.N. Secretary-General was unable to reply to the direct questions asked by the Congolese Prime Minister. In Leopoldville Hammarskjöld engaged in a "business" correspondence with Lumumba's Government from a sumptuous hotel.

We are speaking and writing as though Lumumba were alive, just as we had seen him. A tall and well-made man looks openly at you through glasses with slightly short-sighted eyes.

He speaks in a soft, pleasant voice. He has the manners of an intellectual and the heart of a fighter. After a session in Parliament, when he had to take the floor three times, he rode home to play with his four children. He is a fond father....

It is hard to believe that what happened to Patrice Lumumba took place in the second half of the twentieth century. Just think of it! The lawfully elected Prime Minister of a young African republic was seized by the bandits of the usurper Mobutu, thrown into a dungeon in Thysville and then transported by special plane to Katanga. Regretfully we do not have all the facts of the brutal slaying of Lumumba and his comrades-in-arms, President of the Congolese Senate Joseph Okito and Minister of Defence Maurice Mpolo. But it is obvious that Lumumba's "escape" was a fake and that it was made public after the prisoners of the Katanga jail had been put to death. Could it be that what President Modibo Keita of the Mali Republic spoke of a few days before the terrible news crashed down upon the world was actually what happened? Speaking of the physical reprisal that was being prepared against Lumumba, Keita declared:

"Eight hundred thousand Belgian francs are to be collected in Paris and sent to Brazzaville, from where this money will be taken to the Congo. Hired assassins are to be paid from this first instalment. Lumumba's second escape will be engineered to allow the assassins to commit their crime. It would not be superfluous to recall that during Lumumba's first escape certain Belgian newspapers reported: 'It was stupid to arrest him! We could have settled this devilish problem at once!'"

What was "not settled" at once was done later.

Foreign observers saw Patrice Lumumba and his comrades-in-arms for the last time at the Elisabethville aerodrome on January 17, 1961. They were blindfolded and covered with blood.

No one must forget the condemnatory fact that the U.N. Command in the Congo perpetrated a crime when on two occasions it surrendered and betrayed the head of the legal Government of the Congo Republic: the first time into the hands of Mobutu and Kasavubu, and the second time into the hands of the Belgian aggressors and Tshombe.

Patrice Lumumba never camouflaged his political convictions. On behalf of his Party and on behalf of the Congolese people he demanded the full and final abolition of the colonial system. He never sought a compromise with the imperialists and their creatures. That was why he was hated in colonialist circles. That was why plots were organised against him in Leopoldville and in Brazzaville on the far bank of the Congo.

The murder of Patrice Lumumba shocked the whole world.

Lumumba became a legend, a symbol, a banner of struggle. The whole world now realises the full significance of the loss. Lumumba was not released as was undeviatingly demanded by world public opinion. He was tortured to death. The American *Washington Post and Times Herald* can now stop worrying that "Lumumba's release will be an obvious risk for the Western Powers". We know that behind the Katanga hangmen there are definite "white" faces. Sitting in an international organisation they squeezed out of themselves official "condolences" that sounded as though they were glued together with pieces of gutta-percha.

They will always be haunted by the ghost of the dead hero and martyr! It is time the whole world forcibly declared that the post of U.N. Secretary-General is incompatible with villainy. May the wrath and grief of millions of Congolese and of hundreds of millions of ordinary folks the world over finally force the overt and covert accomplices of the crime in a nameless Katanga village out of their high posts in the U.N.!

Lumumba is no longer among the living. The Congo lost a great son. He perished in the prime of his anti-colonial, patriotic activity. A prime minister may be unlawfully removed and assassinated, but the idea of the Congo's unity cannot be put down. Lumumba is no more. But his staunch supporters and his Party remain. Writing about them, the newspaper *Uhuru* said:

"The Congo National Movement Party is the motor of our entire movement. Its credo and ours is unity.

"Belgium should have realised that the views expressed by Lumumba were the views of the majority of the Congolese people. Lumumba always forestalled the designs of those who shape Belgium's foreign policy. We call upon the entire people to participate in political activity and support the national movement that was created and organised by Lumumba's Party. For those who are fighting for the future of our country we bring to mind a piece of ancient wisdom, which says that the substance of life is not that man should fall, but, on the contrary, that he should continually rise. At this culminating period we call upon you to support unity. History and the people will appraise the efforts we are making today. Long live a united and indivisible Congo! Long live Lumumba and freedom!"

"Lumumba and freedom!", "Lumumba and independent Congo!" are the slogans with which thousands upon thousands of Congolese are rising to the struggle against the Belgian aggressors and their satellites. Lumumba's bright life inspires people to the performance of great deeds. The savage murders are evidence of the agony of the outworn system of slavery. Lumumba's very death is mobilising the Congolese to the struggle for freedom and independence, for the sake of which Africa's national hero Patrice Lumumba lived, worked and suffered with such supreme courage to the last drop of his blood.

Source: Patrice Lumumba, The Truth about a Monstrous Crime of the Colonialists, Moscow, Foreign Languages Publishing House, 1961, pp 105-115.

Written: by N. KHOKHLOV, Izvestia Special Correspondent

Transcribed: by Thomas Schmidt.

Meetings with Lumumba

Romano LEDDA

"You say you are an Italian journalist and wish to get a visa for the Congo? Why do you wish to go there?" those were the first words Patrice Lumumba said to me in Conakry at the residence of Sekou Toure.

Why? It was the beginning of August 1960. The whole world was watching Lumumba, and this man whom nearly two hundred journalists were hunting all over Africa was asking me: "Why?" For more than ten days I had waited in suspense in the hope of finding an aircraft that was going to the Congo from the Guinean capital. I was beginning to grow desperate when Lumumba arrived on his tour of the capitals of African states. I pinned all my hopes on my talk with him and therefore prepared a long speech. With his simple question he made that speech unnecessary, and all I could do was to mumble some words that sounded banal to my own ears.

I watched him as he looked through my papers.... Tall and very thin, the Head of the Congolese Government bore the marks of the suffering he had gone through in prison and of the strain of his present work. The austere black suit gave his elegant figure and his entire appearance a modesty that was devoid of any ostentation. But his face was what really attracted me: small, with a sharp chin and a goatee that made him look wily and even sly, it became unusually naive-looking and good-natured as soon as the lips parted in a broad smile.

And then the eyes. Infinitely lively, they reflected all the anxieties and sufferings of the last months of his life: the sufferings of a prisoner of the Belgians, the pride of the Prime Minister of the Congolese Republic, love for the people, abhorrence of injustice, responsiveness to the pulse of Africa, the fury of struggle, and responsibility before history. It seemed as though one image was superimposed over another, changing the picture of Lumumba that I had brought with me from Europe and my first superficial impressions, but making it impossible as yet to form a firm opinion of him.

> "I'm sorry," he said with a foxy smile, "but unfortunately I cannot give you a visa for the Congo because all the airports are under U.N. control. All I can offer you is to come with me in my aircraft. But you will have to be patient. You will have to follow me to Monrovia, Accra and Lome. We'll go on to the Congo after that."

...It was more than I had hoped for. For nearly three days I travelled with Lumumba and could see him almost at any time I liked. I found that this person, so hated and slandered in the West, was really one of the most generous and most earnest men in the African continent, one of the most courageous fighters and one of the most gifted and modern-thinking leaders of the national, anti-imperialist movement.

* * *

The official reasons for our meetings with Lumumba were the communiqués on talks first with Tubman, then with Nkrumah and, finally, with Sylvanus Olympio. But in the aircraft and after official banquets he frequently looked for us to have a talk, hear our opinions and sometimes, if there was a need for it, to discuss what one or another journalist was planning to write.

In Lome, Togo, for example, we witnessed the political meetings between Lumumba and Olympio. Hostile to any form of "protocol" (but by no means ignoring the importance of the position he occupied), Lumumba wanted us to sit with his delegation in the meeting room, declaring that he had "nothing to hide from the world". That is why, when the talks ended, we remained behind and got into a conversation. Lumumba had recently returned from a visit to the United States, and Tom Brady of *The New York Times* asked him what he thought of the country. Lumumba said he found it a wonderful country and that he had been given a magnificent reception.

"As a matter of fact," he noted, "some centuries ago America fought for her independence against foreigners. It would seem that the Americans should never forget it, but it looks to me as if they are beginning to forget."

"Why do you think so?" Brady asked.

"Look what's happening in the United Nations," Lumumba replied. "We gazed at the world, at the whole world, with trust. I am not a Communist, although you maintain that I am. But America, no matter how things go, is on the side of the colonialists. Perhaps she's not on the side of Belgium, but it's obvious that in using the U.N. she has her eye on our riches. It's like that business over the aircraft, for which I was attacked by newspapermen. I flew to America in a Russian plane. That is true. I asked the Americans for a plane, but they refused to let me have one after procrastinating with their reply for two whole days. What was I to do? I asked the Russians for a plane, and they put one at my disposal in two hours. Now it is said that I am a Communist. But judge for yourself what was more important: to be regarded a Communist or to turn down an opportunity to go to the U.N. to defend our interests there? Judge for yourself."

After this many people said Lumumba was an empiricist, that he manoeuvred wherever he could, turning this way and that, shifting and dodging. I do not share that opinion. At that time he was only learning to administer a state that had risen from nothing, and in everything he did he proceeded from his own perception of the world. Man was the main thing. All else was mystification. All men want to be free, and that is why all people can and must help the Congo. The only "but" here is that this aid must in no way restrict the Congo's freedom.

Pursuing this general line, he trusted everybody, even adventurist businessmen who, seeking publicity, spoke of unreal projects and gave out that they were planning to put money into them. This went on for the first few weeks after he came to power. But later, in August 1960, he began to be more discriminating. This was dictated by the nature of the struggle, whose objective was to win political and economic independence for the country. Neither Tom Brady nor any of the others who called Lumumba a "frenzied Communist" understood this at the time.

Keen, enthusiastic and determined to fulfil his role as leader of the Congolese, Lumumba was a calm person by nature and, despite his youth, inclined to meditation. He was thirty-four, but he was weighted down by the entire burden of seventy-five years of grief, slavery and poverty. He had absorbed into himself, as it were, all of his people's sufferings.

The whole Government came to the aerodrome to meet him when we landed in Leopoldville. A small group of journalists, myself among them, accompanied him to his home. Formerly the residence of the Belgian governor, the house was built in the taste of a Flemish sausage-maker: salons decorated in baroque alternated with small, colonial-style drawing-rooms, and the only really beautiful things in it were the tragic and grotesque totems from the African bush. Lumumba refused to move into one of the magnificent villas built by Belgian businessmen on a hill. He turned the house virtually into a camp, dividing the rooms into living premises and offices.

His wife and three children waited at the entrance. The small woman, who was still unused to the role of wife of a man the whole world was talking about, and the man, who for a moment forgot everything about him, merged in a long and moving embrace. With a happy look on his face he introduced his three children, François, Juliana and Patrice, the eldest, who asked his father if he had brought back a cowboy hat.

A few minutes later (it was about 11 p.m.), Lumumba made a short statement to more than two hundred newsmen about his trip to America and his African tour, and then got the Government together to analyse the situation. The meeting ended at about four in the morning. I later learned that he worked eighteen hours a day, because he had to look into all sorts of problems, even trifling ones. He patiently endeavoured to satisfy all callers.

There were many volumes in his bookcase: speeches by Sekou Toure and Nkrumah, magazines, poetry, and a biography of Simon Kimbangu.

> "All these books," he said, "reached me in the past few years through underground channels. They were our daily bread in the days when we had the luck to be out of prison."

I saw Lumumba nearly every day at his routine press conference. He would walk into the big room, make a short statement and then answer questions for about an hour. At these press conferences each newsman, who was in any way fair, could appreciate Lumumba's statesmanship despite the young Prime Minister's native simplicity and inexperience. He was guided by modern ideas suggested to him by the experience of revolution, which although modern in spirit clashed with the reality that was only just crystallising, with tribal differences, ethnic contradictions, and the grim heritage of colonial rule.

There was, I remember, an amazing press conference in connection with events that disturbed the peace in the city and brought rival tribes into collision. At that press conference Lumumba spoke of national unity, of the honour of being conscious that one was a Congolese and not a Baluba or a Batetela. He spoke of the sacrifices that the people would have to make to create a nation, of the patience that was needed to put an end to the deep-rooted enmity. He was afraid of a war between the Congolese and did his utmost to avert it. That was why he tolerated in his Government even his enemies who were already plotting against him.

* * *

Although these contacts were considerable, each of us wanted to know more, to speak to Lumumba personally, to get interviews from him and learn what was uppermost in his mind. But that was impossible. Pressure of work put him out of our reach.

And yet I had the great luck to see him outside a press conference.

We newsmen were told to come at four o'clock, but the hour hand showed five and still Lumumba did not appear. The newsmen became nervous and grumbled, and one of them, I do not remember who he represented but he was undoubtedly a racialist, declared:

"We can't let a Negro, even if he is a Prime Minister, keep us waiting so long."

There are scoundrels among newspapermen as well.

There were about thirty people, and gradually all of them followed the racialist out of the room. Only an East Berlin correspondent and I stayed behind. Lumumba, who had been informed of everything by his secretary, appeared a few minutes later. I could see he was angry. But he quickly gained control over himself and, courteously asking us to take a seat, said:

> "It's idiotic. Any racialism, white or black, is simply idiotic. I know," he said, turning to me, "that you are a Communist. But that's not the point. You are a cultured person like your comrade here. Tell me, what can I do for you?"

That was when I got my interview.

I got my second close look at Lumumba at the aerodrome in Leopoldville. I was at my hotel when somebody from the office of the Council of Ministers telephoned and told me to drive to the aerodrome. I got there at the same time as Lumumba. With him were General Lundula, Minister for Youth Affairs and Sports Mpolo, and two soldiers. He got out of his car, went to the hangar alone, opened the door and shouted:

"In the name of the Congolese Government you are arrested."

In the hangar were about sixty Belgian paratroopers. They were armed to the teeth and were guarded by U.N. Swedish troops. It was a unique situation. It is quite unusual for a Prime Minister personally to arrest people. And if an unarmed man with only a few companions sets out to arrest armed paratroopers he must be brave as a lion. Lumumba had that courage. It was a sober, conscious courage, a courage that is ruled by common sense and gives birth to true heroism.

There was nothing the Belgians could do. Ten minutes later the stunned paratroopers climbed into a lorry that was waiting for them. Five minutes after they were gone Lumumba laughed over the episode and said:

"If we had decided to wait until this was done by the U.N. Secretary-General, we would have found the paratroopers under our beds."

Although Lumumba called upon his people to have full trust in the U.N. because he wanted to avoid bloodshed, he was perfectly well aware that Hammarskjöld's behaviour was the principal reason for the disorders. Now he was looking for a solution that would not infringe upon the Congo's territorial integrity or restrict its economic and political independence. The solution lay in appealing to the people, in mobilising them and drawing them into direct participation in the Congo's struggle against old and new colonialism.

The Congolese were his people. It seems to me that I never saw Lumumba so happy and confident as when he toured Orientale Province and visited Stanleyville. It was where during the rule of the Belgians Lumumba had struggled, suffered and worked to create the first modern Congolese party that would stand above tribal discord and be linked up with the African national movement. It was where day after day for five years he had trained personnel, established branches of his party in every village and united the entire province around his programme.

* * *

The huge, jubilant crowd of politically mature people that welcomed him on his arrival was different from the crowds in other parts of the Congo. It was a triumph. One could feel that Lumumba had merged with his people. I remember his old father. His face bore the marks of poverty and he had the coarse hands of a man who had hunted for food with bow and arrow. Now these hands embraced the son, who was carried aloft by young people chanting: *"Uhuru*—Freedom!"

On the next day we were in the bush. Women, old men and children poured out of every village to the river bank to celebrate, honour and speak with Lumumba, their "son, the son of the earth, their brother in grief and hope". A long Moslem gown, symbol of authority, was put on him. He laughed, shaking hands with everybody, and in each village he spoke, sang and danced with his people, inviting us to join in the dancing.

That evening he made one of the most important speeches of his short career. Starting a very interesting conversation with the people at the stadium in Stanleyville (the peasants asked questions and he replied, and then he asked them for advice and they gave it), Lumumba spoke of the profound transformations that were needed to place the Congo's enormous wealth into the hands of the people, of the new state system under which tribes had to disappear, of popular initiative and the liberation of Katanga, of the future united and peace-loving Africa. He spoke in Lingala and then translated his words into French for our benefit, for the three or four European newsmen accompanying him.

Other Europeans suddenly appeared in the stadium. They were Belgians who had refused to leave the Congo and wanted to co-operate with Lumumba's Government. With a happy smile, he called them to the rostrum, introduced them to the people as brothers and, addressing us, said:

> "Tell the whole world about this. We are not opposed to white people. We do not mean harm to anybody. People of every colour must be friends. That is our goal."

In the evening we had dinner with him at the residence of the provincial governor. There was nervousness, tension in the air. I was told that important news was expected from Katanga. An hour later we heard a car drive up, and Lumumba started. He rose, ran to the door and cried:

> "They've come!"

They were several Baluba who had arrived from Katanga. In order to slip through the Belgian guards, they had made the journey in an ambulance. Throughout the week's journey they had had only one hour of fresh air at night and several bananas as their entire ration. In rags, hungry, and seeming to fall asleep as they walked, they looked like phantoms. I hurried over to them. The Baluba chief, who was fighting Tshombe, shouted when he saw me with a notebook in my hand:

"We haven't come here for a press conference. Lumumba, we've come for fighting men."

Lumumba embraced each one of them in turn, questioned them and solicitously looked to their needs with a tenderness I never suspected him capable of. And yet such was Lumumba. On the following morning our cars came across a large group of ragged soldiers, with who were women and children. Lumumba stopped his car and wanted to know who they were. They proved to be Congolese soldiers, who had been transferred to Ruanda-Urundi and had refused to serve the Belgians. The Belgians had requisitioned all their property and told them they could walk back to the Congo. It was the first time I saw tears in Lumumba's eyes. He took all the money he had on him, emptied the pockets of his Ministers and gave it all to these people. At the same time, in spite of the financial crisis in the Congo and the shortage of funds, he ordered these people to be given housing and 50,000 francs for immediate needs, and enlisted in the Congolese National Army.

Such was Lumumba. He shared all he had with his people. When he became Prime Minister he did not draw a salary, ate very frugally and in no way took advantage of his high position. Many of the Ministers, of course, did not act in the same way. There were Ministers who spent money right and left (they had never had money before), and frequented luxury cabarets and bars, learning of their existence for the first time. They enjoyed all the blessings of authority, and all of them were on the other side of the fence, with the Belgians, with the colonialists.

I saw how Lumumba lived with my own eyes. One day I went to see a doctor at an out-patient clinic and there met his wife, small Patrice and his driver Maurice, a devoted and intelligent young man. Maurice told me that Lumumba was looking for me. He had been given an Italian magazine rifle and wanted to show it to me. I went to his home and, as usual, found him immersed in a multitude of affairs. He invited me into his flat. It consisted of a tiny room with three beds for the children, another room with a bed, wardrobe and chest of drawers for himself and his wife, a small and very simply furnished dining-room and a kitchen. They had no servants. His wife, a small, pregnant woman, did the cooking for the family and also for

Maurice and Lumumba's brother Louis. They were expecting another child and were thinking of getting another flat. This was Lumumba's only plan for his family.

* * *

Later I saw Lumumba at the All-African Conference in Leopoldville, where he made one of his most magnificent speeches. In it he gave full voice to his nationalist convictions, his all-absorbing love for the Congo and his ideal of a united Africa. One of the phrases sat deep in my mind. I should say it revealed most fully what he felt and wished. He said:

> "We were offered a choice between liberation and the continuation of bondage. There can be no compromise between freedom and slavery. We chose to pay the price of freedom."

The last time I saw him was before my departure from the Congo. It was a Saturday. I went to say good-bye to him and thank him for his assistance. I doubt if he ever knew my name. To him I was simply an Italian journalist, a correspondent of one of the few European newspapers that watched the struggle of the Congolese people with sympathy and understanding.

I found him, as usual, at work. The situation was not very good, but at least it was calm. No one expected a coup d'etat (it took place on Monday). At the time Lumumba was working on two or three decisive problems: the liberation of Katanga, relations with the U.N., and aid from abroad in order to allow the Congo to hold out. Famine was knocking on the door. Lumumba took a few minutes off for a talk with me. He spoke optimistically of the future. He had profound faith in people. I wished him every success and a long life. Once more he told me that his life was of no importance whatever but that he was firmly convinced that no Congolese would ever raise his hand against him.

"We are all blood brothers."

His last words to me were:

"You will probably come back to the Congo and we'll meet again. You will find a free, rich and flourishing country with no survivals of slavery."

That is what he wanted most of all, and for that he was murdered.

Source: Patrice Lumumba: Fighter for Africa 's Freedom, *Moscow, Progress Publishers, 1961, pp 93-104.* ***Written:*** *by Romano LEDDA, Italian journalist;* ***Transcribed:*** *by Thomas Schmidt.*

Brick Memorial erected for Lumumba, who was buried with two other men in a shallow grave at this site. The bodies were later removed and destroyed.

The evergreen in Congo's Katanga province, where Lumumba was shot.

Patrice Lumumba, Stanleyville, May 1960 by D'Lynn Waldron ©

FOLLOWING PAGES ARE INTENTIONALLY LEFT BLANK FOR NOTES